Roads
Less Traveled
IN NORTHWEST OREGON I

A Guide to Back Roads and Special Places

Second Edition

(signature)

Steve Arndt

About the Roads Less Traveled Series:

"The series will stitch together the state's history and habitat for anyone who pays as much attention to what they're driving through as where they're going." — **Bill Monroe, *The Oregonian***

---

www.roadslesstraveledoregon.com

Also by Steve Arndt:

Roads Less Traveled in Northeast Oregon
Roads Less Traveled in Northwest Oregon II
Roads Less Traveled in North-Central Oregon
Roads Less Traveled in Southeast Oregon
Roads Less Traveled in South-Central Oregon
Roads Less Traveled in Southwest Oregon

Roads Less Traveled in Northwest Oregon I, Second Edition
A Guide to Back Roads and Special Places

Steve Arndt

Photographs by
Diane Arndt of Woodburn, Oregon

Maps by
Justin Eslinger, Box Lunch Design

Printed in the United States of America

ISBN: 978-0-9844294-3-1

Front Cover:
    Road less traveled near Hebo Lake
    (Photograph by Diane Arndt)

Back Cover (from top to bottom)
    House in Perrydale
    Oregon Electric Booster Station near Pirtle
    Barn near Yamhill
    Viewpoint near Astoria
    Thompson Flouring Mill in Shedd
    (Photographs by Diane Arndt)

Designed by

Justin Eslinger | Box Lunch Design
boxlunchdesign@gmail.com

Dedicated to

William Gilbaugh

Friend, father figure, fellow traveler, and inspiration
behind this series of books.

I shall be telling this with a sigh
Somewhere ages and ages hence:
Two roads diverged in a wood, and I—
I took the one less traveled by,
And that has made all the difference.

—Robert Frost (1874-1963)
from his poem, "The Road Not Taken"

Acknowledgements

Special Thanks to:

My good friends from the Woodburn United Methodist Church
who ran routes and double-checked mileage

Warner Pacific College
who granted me the sabbatical that allowed me the time to travel, research, and write this book

Lou and Myra Folz
dear friends, for their company and camaraderie on road trips

Sheridan City Hall and its employees
who gladly gave of their time and resources in order to assist us in securing information about their city

Lucy Hebert
Sheridan Realtor who proudly shared about her community

Kris Gullo
Manager of the McMinnville Downtown Association for mailing important information and dates regarding her city

The following Chambers of Commerce, Visitors Centers, Museums, and numerous people from the communities listed below, who contributed information for this book:

Albany	Amity	Astoria
Banks	Birkenfeld-Mist	Brownsville
Carlton	Clatskanie	Cloverdale
Falls City	Forest Grove	Gaston
Harrisburg	Jefferson	Marcola
McMinnville	Stayton	Summit
Sweet Home	Vernonia	Willamina
Yamhill		

All who provided assistance in the production of this book or shared information about their communities and with sincere apologies to anyone not mentioned by name.

Contents

Introduction   i

All Aboard:
The Oregon Electric Line   **1**
Albany to Junction City (51 miles)

    Albany   3
    Pirtle   6
    Riverside   7
    Orleans   8
    Verdure   9
    Oakville   10
    Peoria   11
    Fayetteville   12
    Shedd   13
    Halsey   15
    Harrisburg   17
    Junction City   19

Covered Bridges and Sacred Cows   **21**
Jefferson to Lebanon (67 Miles)

    Jefferson   23
    Marion   25
    North Santiam   26
    West Stayton   27
    Stayton   28
    Jordan   31
    Scio   33
    Shelburn   34
    West Scio   35
    Crabtree   37
    Lebanon   39

City Lights, Country Sites,
Mountain Views, Ocean Blues   **41**
Banks to Pacific City (92 miles)

    Banks   43
    Forest Grove   44
    Dilley   47
    Gaston   48
    Yamhill   50
    Carlton   51
    Lafayette   53
    McMinnville   54
    Bellevue   58
    Sheridan   59
    Willamina   61
    Blaine   64
    Beaver   65
    Hebo   66
    Cloverdale   67
    Pacific City   68

It's a Long Way to Apiary   **69**
Buxton to Astoria (111 miles)

    Buxton   71
    Vernonia   72
    Apiary   76
    Alston   77
    Mayger   78
    Clatskanie   79
    Mist   80
    Birkenfeld   82
    Jewell   83
    Olney   84
    Astoria   85

How Green is Kings Valley?   **89**
Dayton to Kernville (135 miles)

    Dayton   91
    Whiteson   93
    Amity   94
    Ballston   96
    Perrydale   97
    Dallas   98
    Falls City   100
    Airlie   103
    Pedee   104
    Kings Valley   105
    Hoskins   106
    Wren   107
    Blodgett   108
    Summit   109
    Nashville   110
    Logsden   111
    Siletz   112
    Kernville   114

Meet Your Waterloo near Berlin   **115**
Lebanon to Coburg (74 miles)

    Lebanon   117
    Sodaville   119
    Waterloo   120
    Berlin   121
    Sweet Home   122
    Holley   124
    Crawfordsville   125
    Brownsville   126
    Mabel   129
    Wendling   130
    Marcola   131
    Mohawk   132
    Coburg   133

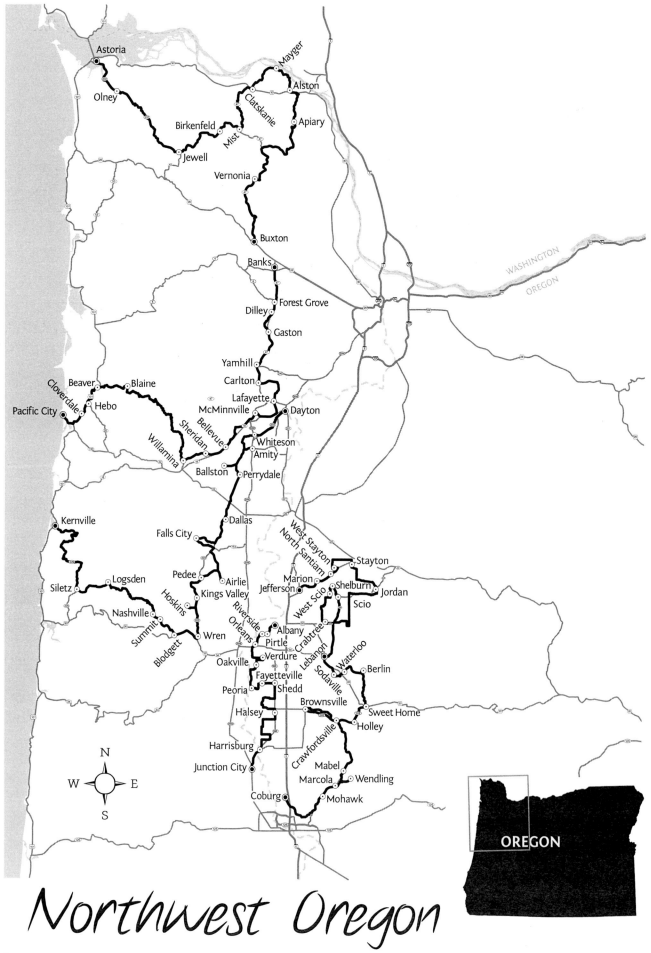

Northwest Oregon

Introduction

As a young boy growing up in Independence during Oregon's centennial, I became fascinated by our state's history, culture and particularly, the smaller, out of the way, once thriving communities. Living within fifteen miles of Buena Vista, Airlie, Suver, King's Valley, Pedee, Falls City, Talbot, and Rickreall added to this curiosity.

Why, I wondered, would some communities thrive and others cease to exist? Why did Salem grow, prosper and become the state capitol and not Buena Vista? Why did Independence, an important Willamette River port and former "Hop Capital of the World," not blossom and grow into a major agricultural and industrial center?

When she was three years old, my daughter would always ask during trips, "Daddy, how much farther, how longer?" My six year old son would then quip, "Are we there yet? I think my freshness date is about to expire!" Similar words are commonly echoed in many cars as families hastily and purposefully scurry to their destinations.

Freeways bypass much of Oregon's rich history. Travelers driving the speed limit are in the minority. The beauty and wonder of our great state are frequently missed because of the frenetic pace we live. This series of books invites people to slow down, visit new places and view our state with a different lens as it guides people along Oregon's often forgotten paths.

One personal example makes my point. Eugene has been a destination many times in my more than fifty years as an Oregonian,

yet I did not know the communities of Pirtle, Orleans, Oakville, Potter and Fayetteville, which lie along roads that parallel Interstate 5 existed. I was amazed to learn that the oldest working water-powered grist mill west of the Mississippi still produces flour and is only a stone's throw from a road that carries 50,000 passengers a day.

Each trip in this book is theme based, between 50 to 150 miles in length, and geared for passage by any vehicle. A few gravel roads along the routes are well maintained and clearly delineated. Many locations are indicated via GPS longitude and latitude coordinates. The availability of gas, food and lodging are indicated for each community. Directions and mile markers are included to help travelers navigate, with potential points of interest identified, both along the routes and in the communities. Side trips are frequently outlined and digression is encouraged.

More importantly, I hope the reader will use this book both as a guide and springboard to explore the many less traveled roads that criss-cross our state, connecting small towns and communities.

At one time Oregon's tourism theme was – *Things Look Differently Here!* I hold this mantra is high regard. It is my hope that people will slow down, take the roads less traveled, learn about our wondrous state, and become acutely aware of its history, its struggles and the ways of life that once existed. Let this book rekindle the pioneer spirit that exists in all Oregonians. And remember – always take the roads less traveled; it could make all the difference.

Steve Arndt

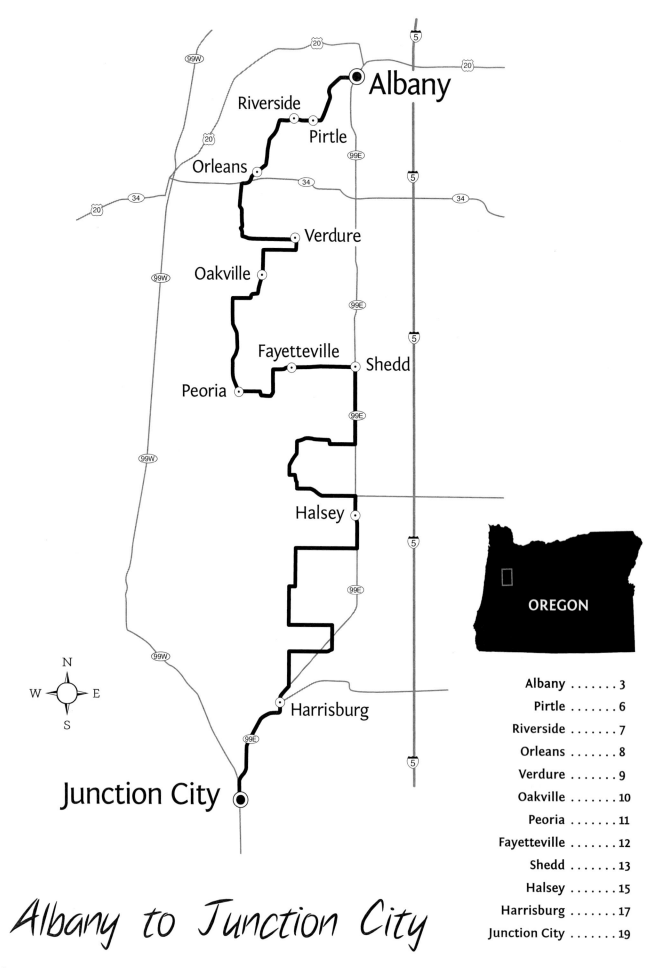

Albany 3

Pirtle 6

Riverside 7

Orleans 8

Verdure 9

Oakville 10

Peoria 11

Fayetteville 12

Shedd 13

Halsey 15

Harrisburg 17

Junction City 19

Albany to Junction City

All Aboard:
The Oregon Electric Railroad Line

Albany to Junction City (51 miles)

The Willamette Valley is a scenic patchwork lined by rivers, creeks, roads and railroad tracks. The Oregon Electric Railroad, which once extended from Portland to Eugene, served the valley from about 1905 until the Great Depression. The Albany to Eugene section was completed in 1912. Electric booster stations, strategically located every five to seven miles along the tracks, supplied electricity to overhead lines that powered the trains as they slowly rambled up and down the valley.

Small communities, including Pirtle, Orleans, Peoria, Munson and Cartney, sprang up around these stations. Eventually, powerful diesel engine trains, designed for strength and long hauls, replaced the electric trains. Consequently, the smaller communities that flourished along the electric rails died. Several concrete booster and ticket stations can be seen along this route that parallels Interstate 5.

The route begins in Albany, once the location of the state capital, and ends in Junction City, which once boasted the finest opera house north of San Francisco and west of the Mississippi River.

Oregon Electric Railroad Booster Station near Halsey

Albany

Elevation: 202 feet

Location:
44.63.018 N • 123.06.092 W

Services:
gas, food, lodging, B&B, RV

Located at the confluence of the Calapooia and Willamette rivers, Albany is a largely farming and manufacturing based city. Squatters Abner Hackelman and Hiram Snead sold their 1845 claim to brothers Walter and Thomas Monteith for the huge sum of $400. The brothers named the town Albany after their beloved home in New York. Hackelman and Snead lived in a log home that would have been located at the corner of 1st and Ellsworth. In 1849, the Monteith's built Albany's first frame house at 518 2nd Avenue, which still stands today. In early 1850, Abram Hackelman, son of Abner, laid out seventy acres on the east side

Albany State Bank

of Albany for future development. At that time, Albany's population totaled nearly 1,000 – mostly farmers who worked the fertile valley soil. Albany's first store opened in 1849, followed by the post office in 1850, the first school in 1851 (located at the corner of 4th and Broadalbin), and the first flourmill in 1852. The first ferry, located at the foot of Ferry Street, began operations in 1851 and was replaced by a steel bridge in 1892. The courthouse was constructed in 1852, the same year the first steamboat successfully made its way up the Willamette River to town. By 1866, five riverboats made regular trips from Albany to Corvallis and Portland. River travel burgeoned in 1870 and travel from Portland to Albany cost one dollar. The first newspaper, *The Oregon Democrat*, began printing news in 1859 and is known today as *The Albany Democrat Herald*. Chinese laborers hand-dug the Santiam Canal that flows through the historic Hackelman district following their arrival in 1884. The first train arrived in 1871 and the railroad line grew to include the world's longest wooden railroad drawbridge (1888). By 1910 over 25 trains per day departed from Albany to various destinations. Waterpower from the canal provided power to run sawmills and flourmills. Electricity was first generated in 1887 and was made available to homes in 1908. The first airport was built in 1909 and in 1910 John Burkhart built the first Aeroplane constructed in Oregon. Albany, the Linn County seat of government, has over 700 buildings in the Downtown, Hackelman, Montieth and Aviation districts listed on the National Historical Registry. Summers in Albany are particularly busy with annual events including tours of historic homes, the Linn County Fair, the Willamette River Festival, and Northwest Art and Air Festival, a three-day gathering of hot air balloons. The revived Albany Timber Carnival is known as the largest logging event on earth. Champion and novice loggers from around the globe compete with their Pacific Northwest counterparts in a variety of lumberjack skills.

Points of Interest

(only a partial listing)

- **Albany Carousel and Museum** (*1st and Washington*)
  Restoration of carousel horses.

- **Rialto Theater** (*111 1st*)
  Circa 1889. Originally a cigar store and billiard hall.

- **Woolworth Building** (*140 1st*)
  Initially a barbershop.

- **Albany State Bank** (*201-203 1st*)
  1908. A sign above the door indicates its origin.

- **Revere House** (*202-204 1st*)
  An 1877 Hotel.

- **Millinery and Insurance Shop** (*209-211 1st*)
  Opened in 1889 as a saloon.

- **First National Bank** (*222 1st*)
  Financed in 1887 by Judge Flinn.

- **Stetter's Grocery** (*211 2nd*)
  The Stetter family lived upstairs in this 1913 building.

- **Post Office** (*240 2nd*)
  Opened in 1914.

- **Blacksmith Shop** (*456 2nd*)
  Operated from 1897 to 1942.

- **Montieth House** (*518 2nd*)
  Built in 1849, the first framed home in Albany.

- **Young's Clothing Store** (*124 Broadalbin*)
  1912.

- **First Savings Bank** (*2nd and Broadalbin*)
  The bank opened in 1909.

- **Sales Sample Store** (*211 Broadalbin*)
  Constructed in 1899.

- **S.E. Young Store** (*163 Lyon*)
  1912 clothing store.

Avery Mill

- **Montieth Park** (*100 Water*)
  Gazebo, stage, picnic, and restrooms.

- **Avery Mill** (*213 Water*)
  This 1866 building is the oldest structure on the river. Train and steamboat tickets were sold here.

- **St. Paul's Methodist Church** (*238 3rd*)
  1868. The steeple has been removed.

- **Bligh Theater** (*231-239 1st*)
  1914. A cigar factory was located in the SW corner of the building.

- **Linn County Bank** (*327 1st*)
  Opened in 1886 and failed in the Depression.

- **Kohn and Company Building** (*415-421 1st*)
  Oldest brick building in Albany. In 1866 it housed a photographer, barber, insurance agent and an undertaker.

- **Albany Chamber of Commerce** (*435 1st*)
  Lots of information available.

- **Albany Grocery and Mercantile** (*442 1st*)
  Two-stories in 1893. Look for the original steel shutters.

- **Former Saloon** (*202 2nd*)
  Today Tripp and Tripp Realty. Built in 1893.

- **Victorian Home** (*323 2nd*)
  Built in 1892 and remodeled in 1982. A livery stable was in the basement.

- **First Printing Office** (*327 2nd*)
  T.L. Alexander opened the business in 1900.

- **Dannal's Furniture Store** (*401-411-413 2nd*)
  Constructed in 1877.

Linn County Courthouse

Albany

Points of Interest (continued)

- **Mill Worker Houses**
  (704-712-718 3rd)
  All of these 1889 homes have identical porches.

- **Linn County Courthouse**
  (4th and Broadalbin)
  Dates to the 1850s.

- **J.B. Wyatt House** *(240 4th)*
  An 1865 Gothic Revival home.

- **Samuel Althouse House**
  (118 5th)
  1868.

- **Train Depot** *(133 5th)*
  In 1912 this was part of the Oregon Electric Line.

- **Albany Regional Museum**
  (136 Lyon)
  Lots of unusual items.

- **Charles Wolverton House**
  (810 Lyon)
  Built for Oregon's Chief Justice in 1889.

- **Baker House** *(606 Baker)*
  Constructed in 1875.

- **John Ralston House**
  (632 Baker)
  An 1889 Eastlake style home.

- **Old Houses**
  (618-624-630 Buhl)
  All built in the 1890s.

- **N.H. Allen House** *(208 6th)*
  Constructed about 1880.

- **Goltra House**
  (331 Montgomery)
  1893 construction.

John Ralston House

bridges over the Willamette River

Albany to Pirtle

Distance:
2.9 miles

Directions:
From the old city center, travel south on Pacific Blvd. (Hwy. 99) to Queen. Turn right on Queen toward Pirtle.

Points En Route

(mileage from Queen and Pacific/Highway 99)

1.3 miles:
Queen becomes Oakville Road.

2.5 miles:
Turn right, traveling west on Pirtle Road.

2.9 miles:
Pirtle

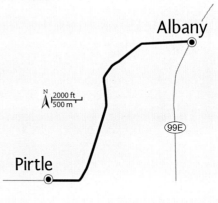

Pirtle

Elevation: 217 feet

Location:
44.35.902 N • 123.08.115 W

Services:
none

Named in honor of Grant Pirtle, an Albany Hotel owner and early settler who owned property near the railroad station, the town was an important stop on the Oregon Electric Railroad. Today, the Oregon Electric booster station and depot are all that remain of this small Linn County community that once had a school, pharmacy, grocery store, and many homes. The concrete booster station is located about 100 yards south of Pirtle Road along the tracks. "OE," an abbreviation of Oregon Electric, is chiseled in the building's cornices. Communities named Pirtle also exist in Oklahoma and Texas.

Electric Booster Station

Points of Interest

- **Electric Booster Station**
  (100 yards from the road)
  The twelve-inch thick concrete walled structure was built almost 100 years ago.

- **Pirtle Lake** *(1.1 miles)*
  A four-acre lake on private property.

Pirtle to Riverside

Distance:
  0.7 miles

Directions:
  From the railroad tracks, proceed west on Pirtle Drive.

Points En Route
(mileage from the railroad tracks)

0.4 miles:
  Cluster of homes.

0.7 miles:
  Riverside

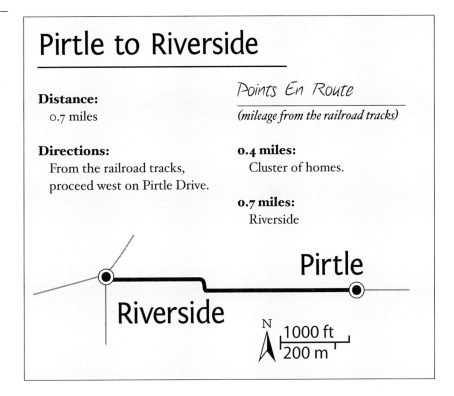

Riverside

Elevation: 223 feet

Location:
44.36.240 N • 123.09.271 W

Services:
none

The name Riverside is descriptive of the community's location near the Willamette River. Another Oregon community named Riverside is located in Malhuer County on the south fork of the Malhuer River. Riverside, Linn County, was denied postal approval because the Eastern Oregon community was named first. A Head Start center now occupies the old Riverside School building.

Points of Interest

- **Riverside Community Hall**
  (35283 Riverside)
  The hub of community activity.

- **Riverside School**
  (corner of Riverside and Pirtle)
  Circa 1930.

- **Bowers Rocks State Park**
  (1.0 miles north on Riverside)
  On the Willamette Greenway, accessible by car and boat.

Riverside Community Hall

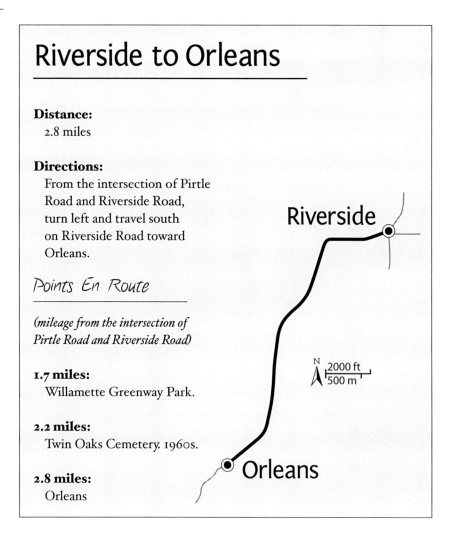

Riverside to Orleans

Distance:
2.8 miles

Directions:
From the intersection of Pirtle Road and Riverside Road, turn left and travel south on Riverside Road toward Orleans.

Points En Route

(mileage from the intersection of Pirtle Road and Riverside Road)

1.7 miles:
Willamette Greenway Park.

2.2 miles:
Twin Oaks Cemetery. 1960s.

2.8 miles:
Orleans

Orleans

Elevation: 233 feet

Location:
44.34.139 N • 123.11.212 W

Services:
none

Orleans was established in 1849 on the Moore family donation land claim. Because the area was prone to flooding, all homes and businesses were wiped out by the terrible 1860s flood except the old school, church, and cemetery.

Points of Interest

- **Orleans Cemetery**
  The land was donated by the Cushman family and dates to the 1850s.

- **Orleans Chapel**
  Across from the cemetery, the chapel is more than 100 years old.

- **Orleans School**
  (1/4 mile south of the cemetery)
  Converted to a private residence.

Orleans to Verdure

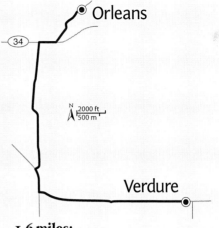

Distance:
4.9 miles

Directions:
From the intersection of Orleans and Riverside, proceed south on Riverside Road.

Points En Route

(mileage from the intersection of Orleans and Riverside)

0.3 miles:
Old mill.

0.5 miles:
Intersection with Highway 34. Turn right on Highway 34, traveling toward Corvallis.

0.7 miles:
Turn left onto White Oak Road.

1.6 miles:
Old farmhouse.

2.5 miles:
Intersection of White Oak and Peoria. Turn left on Peoria Road.

2.8 miles:
Turn left on Tangent Road.

3.8 miles:
Intersection of Tangent and Oakville Road. Keep left. Tangent Road and Oakville Road join here for 0.6 miles.

4.4 miles:
Veer right on Tangent Drive at Verdure Western Star Grange.

4.9 miles:
Railroad tracks and outbuildings indicate the site of Verdure.

Orleans Chapel

Verdure

Elevation: 241 feet

Location:
44.31.579 N • 123.09.395 W

Services:
none

Verdure was an important stop on the Oregon Electric Railway. First called Oakville, the name changed to Verdure in 1916 because a nearby community had already registered the name. A single, large warehouse, the nearby Western Star Grange, and scattered farmhouses make up Verdure today. Another community named Verdure exists in Utah.

Points of Interest

- **Warehouse**
  (adjacent to RR tracks)
  Grain and Seed Storage.

- **Western Star Grange**
  (30423 Tangent Drive)
  Grange #309 has an Albany address.

Western Star Grange

Verdure to Oakville

Distance:
 2.7 miles

Directions:
 At the tracks, continue east on Tangent Rd.

Points En Route

(mileage from the tracks)

0.1 miles:
 Turn right, heading south on Country Road.

0.4 miles:
 Turn right on Harvest Drive (gravel).

0.6 miles:
 Crossing railroad tracks.

1.2 miles:
 Pavement returns.

1.6 miles:
 Intersection of Harvest and Oakville. Go left on Oakville Road.

1.8 miles:
 Keep left on Oakville Road.

2.1 miles:
 Oakville Cemetery. The cemetery is located on the site of the Maley School, where Reverend Thomas Kendall started preaching in 1850. His 1870 gravesite is the exact location of the pulpit as it stood in the old schoolhouse.

2.7 miles:
 Oakville

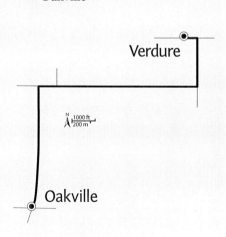

Oakville

Elevation: 242 feet

Location:
44.30.817 N • 123.11.182 W

Services:
none

Oakville was named for the abundance of oak trees that grow in the area. The post office opened in 1878 and closed in 1902, the same year rural delivery began in Oregon. The new Oakville Church, constructed in 1878, is located at the intersection of Oakville Road and Church Road. Reverend Thomas Kendall started preaching here in 1850.

Points of Interest

- **Oakville Presbyterian Church**
  (29970 Church Road)
  Built in 1878. Prior to construction of the new building, services were held in the old Maley School, which was located in what is now the Oakville Cemetery.

- **Old Oakville School**
  (now the church manse)
  Built in 1922.

Oakville
Presbyterian
Church

Oakville to Peoria

Distance:
  5.1 miles

Directions:
  From the intersection of Church and Oakville Road, continue south on Oakville Road toward Peoria.

Points En Route

(mileage from the intersection of Church and Oakville)

0.6 miles:
  Sublime Thyme Gardens. Crossing Muddy Creek. A narrow road winds through wheat fields.

1.8 miles:
  Turn left onto Peoria Road, which follows the Willamette River.

2.2 miles:
  Century Farm.

5.0 miles:
  Peoria County Park. Picnic, rest rooms, boat launch, fishing, limited camping. The old highway cuts through the park.

5.1 miles:
  Peoria

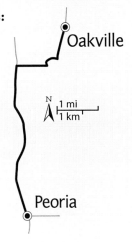

Peoria

Elevation: 256 feet

Location:
44.44.918 N • 123.19.632 W

Services:
none

Peoria, originally called Burlington when the post office opened in 1855, is a sleepy community platted on a hill above the Willamette River near Lake Creek. The name was changed in 1857 to Peoria, after a town in Illinois. The community once prospered with four grain warehouses that stored over 60,000 bushels of wheat during harvest. A toll ferry operated near the Peoria Bible Church.

Victorian House

Points of Interest

- **Peoria New Hope Community Church** (*Main and Peoria Road*) Circa 1900.

- **Old Seed and Grain Warehouse** (*Main and Clay*) Uniquely converted to a residence. Nicely restored and maintained.

- **Victorian House** (*Main and Abraham*) Under restoration.

Peoria to Fayetteville

Distance:
3.1 miles

Directions:
At the intersection of Abraham Drive and Peoria Road, go east on Abraham toward Fayetteville.

Points En Route

(mileage from the intersection of Abraham and Peoria)

1.4 miles:
Turn left on Peckenpaugh Road.

2.3 miles:
Turn right on Fayetteville Drive.

2.5 miles:
Crossing Muddy Creek.

3.1 miles:
Fayetteville

Fayetteville

N 2000 ft / 500 m

Peoria

New Hope Community Church

Fayetteville

Elevation: 256 feet

Location:
44.27.671 N • 123.09.467 W

Services:
none

Fayetteville is located at the inter-section of Pugh Road and Fayette-ville Drive. Southern sympathizers settled here in the 1850s, naming the community after their home in Arkansas. Fayetteville grew around the Oregon Electric Railroad. It is a major distribution point with several grain elevators and grain storage warehouses.

Points of Interest

• **Pugh Cemetery**
  (across from the grain elevators)
  Headstones date to the late 1800s.

grain elevator in Fayetteville

Fayetteville to Shedd

Distance:
  2.5 miles

Directions:
  Proceed east on Fayetteville Drive.

Points En Route

(mileage from the railroad tracks)

2.1 miles:
  Teen Challenge Training Center.

2.5 miles:
  Shedd

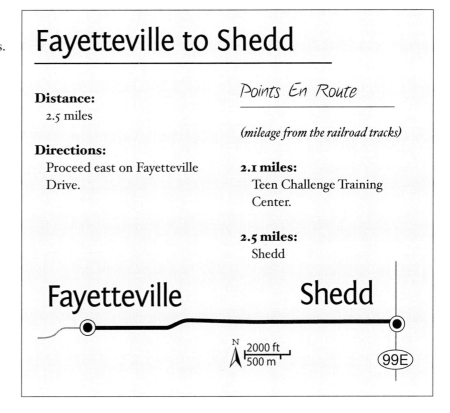

Shedd

Elevation: 266 feet

Location:
44.27.237 N • 123.06.524 W

Services:
gas, food

The community of Boston grew around the 1858 gristmill that was established approximately one and a half miles from the present community of Shedd. The Boston community was platted in 1861 and was designed to resemble a New England-style town square. It soon became an important stagecoach stop. The Boston Mills post office opened in 1869 and the name changed to Shedd's Station in 1871, named after Captain Frank Shedd who donated land for the community. The railroad arrived in 1871, missing the Boston Mill by a mile and a half. All of the buildings in Boston Mills (except for the gristmill) were moved to be near the railroad tracks. In 1899, the railroad changed the name of the newly formed community to Shedd. The Boston Mill, also known as Thompson's Flour Mill, is powered by water from the Calapooia River.

Boston Mill

Points of Interest

- **Porter-Brasfield House**
  (*31838 Fayetteville Dr*)
  The oldest home in Shedd.

- **Shedd Presbyterian Church**
  (*30045 Highway 99E*)
  Constructed in 1892.

- **United Methodist Church**
  (*30090 Highway 99E*)
  A congregation was established in 1853 and the church opened in 1873. Look for the old bell in the tower.

- **Shedd Museum** (*29990 1st*)
  The museum is housed in a former bank building.

- **Shedd Store** (*B and Highway 99*)
  The original store was moved to this location from Brownsville.

- **Masonic Lodge** (*between B and C streets on Highway 99E*)
  A grand structure with impressive columns.

- **Shedd Café**
  (*30005 Hwy. 99E*)
  Known for its burgers and classic car rallies.

Masonic Lodge

- **W.O.W. Building**
  (D and Highway 99E)
  The Woodsman of the World Lodge is a vacant and boarded two-story building.

- **Railroad Avenue**
  A collection of older houses parallel the east side of the railroad tracks.

- **Shedd Cemetery**
  (3/4 mile south of town)
  Established in the 1880s.

- **Boston Mill**
  (1.8 miles on Boston Mill Road)
  Also called Thompson's Flour Mill, the area is now a state park. It is the oldest, continuously running, water powered mill in Oregon. Only four gristmills remain in Oregon. This is one of two that are still in operation. Guided tours during the summer.

- **Mill Keeper's House**
  (in the State Park)
  The home was constructed in 1904 and the Carriage House in 1902.

- **Bunker Hill Cemetery**
  (on the hill across from the mill)
  Also dates to the late 1800s.

Shedd Presbyterian Church

Shedd to Halsey

Distance:
9.7 miles

Directions:
From the intersection of B Street and Highway 99E, go south on 99E.

Points En Route

(mileage from the Shedd Market at the intersection of B Street and Highway 99E)

0.2 miles:
An old gas station.

0.8 miles:
Shedd Cemetery, established in 1853.

0.9 miles:
Pugh Farms. 1912.

2.8 miles:
Turn right on Oak Plain Drive.

4.4 miles:
Oak Farm Seed and Processing. 1850.

4.5 miles:
Crossing Muddy Creek.

5.2 miles:
Site of Potter, a stop along the Oregon Electric Line.

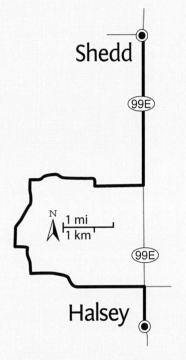

5.2 miles:
Intersection of Oak Plain and Potter. Turn left on Potter.

6.5 miles:
Intersection of Potter and Creek Bend Road. Turn left on Creek Bend.

7.3 miles:
Intersection of Creek Bend and American Drive. Go left on American Drive toward Halsey.

9.7 miles:
Halsey

Halsey

Elevation: 289 feet

Location:
44.38.411 N • 123.10.809 W

Services:
gas, food

While settlers lived in the area for two decades, the community was not founded until 1872, the same year the railroad arrived. The city incorporated in 1876. Halsey was named after William Halsey, vice president of the Willamette Valley Railroad. On July 31, 1903, a fire swept through the downtown, destroying most of the buildings. Halsey farmers, aided by cool temperatures and over forty-five inches of yearly rain, grow high quality grass seed.

Wooden Grain Elevator

Points of Interest

- **Halsey Train Depot** (*Halsey Street across from the post office*)
  The depot is reportedly the second oldest in the valley. The 1880 building was moved to this site in 2000.

- **Post office** (*745 1st*)
  Formerly the Halsey Bank.

- **City Hall** (*773 1st*)
  Next to the Halsey bank.

- **Former Halsey Grocery** (*891 1st*)
  Across from the grain elevator.

- **Wooden Grain Elevator** (*1st and D*)
  Survived the fire.

- **Central Linn Elementary School** (*239 W 2nd*)
  The hub of the community.

- **Halsey United Methodist Church** (*611 3rd*)
  More than 100 years old.

- **Old Houses**
  (*817 3rd and 1365 3rd*)
  Each constructed more than 100 years ago.

- **Doctors House** (*791 4th*)
  Note the second entrance, used by patients.

- **Grace Bible Community Church** (*411 Main*)
  Built after the fire.

- **Halsey Memorial Park**
  (*on Highway 99 between O and L*)
  The park was dedicated in 1899. Picnic, play, restrooms.

Grace Bible Community Church

Halsey to Harrisburg

Distance:
12.8 miles

Directions:
From the Halsey Park at O and Highway 99, go south on Highway 99E.

Points En Route

(mileage from O and Highway 99E)

1.2 miles:
Turn right on Lake Creek Lane.

3.6 miles:
Turn left on Malpass Road.

4.6 miles:
Site of Nixon. A station on the Oregon Electric Railroad, Nixon was named for early settler Samuel Nixon.

6.8 miles:
Intersection of Malpass and Cartney Roads. Turn left, heading east, on Cartney Road to continue the route, noting that the site of Cartney and a 1912 Oregon Electric Booster Station are located 0.2 miles west of this intersection (30214 Cartney). Cartney was named for J.M. Cartney who owned the land on which the train station was constructed. The station is now part of a grain storage complex. Former railroad worker housing is located at 30366 Cartney.

8.5 miles:
Turn right on Powerline Road.

8.9 miles:
Alford Cemetery, dates to 1853. Stay on Powerline, crossing highway 99E and RR tracks. Alford was a station on the Southern Pacific Railroad line named after 1850 settler Thomas Alford upon whose land the tracks were laid. Alford was originally called Muddy because it was near Muddy Creek. The post office opened in 1874 under the name Muddy Station. It closed about one year later. The name of the community was changed to Alford about 1900.

9.1 miles:
The IOOF and Masonic Cemeteries. The twin cemeteries date to the 1850s.

9.4 miles:
Woodsman Cemetery, 1885.

9.5 miles:
Turn right on Substation Road.

9.9 miles:
Crossing railroad tracks and 99E. Continue west on Subdivision Road.

11.1 miles:
Turn left on Tandy Lane.

12.5 miles:
Turn right on Highway 99E.

12.8 miles:
Harrisburg

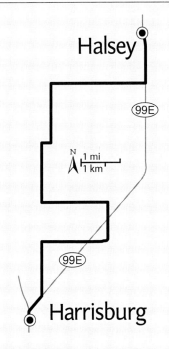

O.E. Booster Station in Cartney

Harrisburg

Elevation: 312 feet

Location:
44.16.872 N • 123.10.065 W

Services:
gas, food, lodging, RV

Named after Harrisburg, Pennsylvania in 1853, the area was briefly called Prairie Precinct and then Thurston. The post office opened in 1855 as Thurston but closed a year later when the name was officially changed to Harrisburg. The town was incorporated in 1866. Harrisburg was as far south as steamboats could navigate on the Willamette River.

Steam Boat Park

Points of Interest

- **Old Town Harrisburg**
  (between 1st and 7th and Territorial Road and La Salle)
  Many old buildings, the ferry landing, steamboat landing and two city parks are located in this part of town.

- **Fire Hall** *(172 Smith)*
  Circa 1880.

- **Harrisburg Bank** *(195 Smith)*
  Built in 1887 and known as the Rampy Bank. The safe is visible through the windows.

- **Steam Boat Park** *(1st and Smith)*
  The pavilion in the park marks the location of the old steamboat landing.

- **Victorian Mansion**
  (2nd and LaSalle)
  A large, elegant home constructed about 1888.

- **Old Church** *(2nd and Kesling)*
  Closed and forgotten.

- **Ferry Landing**
  (Highway 99E bridge)
  The ferry operated from 1848 until 1925, when the bridge was constructed.

- **VFW Hall** *(160 Smith)*
  A small, plain building.

- **Cartwright Building**
  (262 Smith)
  Built in the 1920s.

- **Harrisburg Park** *(4th and Smith)*
  Picnic.

Victorian Mansion

- **Harrisburg Skate Park**
  (530 Smith)
  Lots of concrete, dips and rails.

- **Harrisburg Christian Church**
  (Smith and 6th)
  The church opened in the
  early 1900s.

- **Harrisburg Museum**
  (near the Christian Church)
  A series of several buildings
  that provide much local history.
  Included is J.M. McCartney's 1867
  pioneer residence, an old caboose,
  a chapel and old outbuildings,
  all brought to this site. The old
  Harrisburg school bell hangs from
  a pole near the entrance to the
  museum.

- **Harrisburg United Methodist
  Church** *(710 7th)*
  Over a century old.

- **Physician's House** *(7th)*
  Note the two doors, one for the
  family and one for patients.

Harrisburg to Junction City

Distance:
  3.2 miles

Directions:
  Travel southwest on highway
  99E.

Points En Route

*(mileage from 2nd and Highway 99E
near the bridge)*

0.1 miles:
  Crossing the Willamette River.

1.4 miles:
  Lancaster. Named after
  Lancaster, Pennsylvania, the
  town never incorporated.
  Lancaster was a major river and
  steamboat port until the major
  flooding in the 1860s, which
  changed the course of the
  Willamette River and increased
  the importance of Harrisburg
  as a shipping point. Prior to the
  flood, Lancaster was a larger
  community than Harrisburg.

3.2 miles:
  Junction City

chapel at Harrisburg Museum

Physician's House

Rampy Bank

Junction City

Elevation: 328 feet

Location:
44.12.713 N • 123.12.387 W

Services:
gas, food, lodging, RV

In 1870, under the direction of Ben Holladay, Junction City was scheduled to become the terminus for an east (of the Willamette) and west (of the Willamette) railroad line. Although the east-west railroad was never constructed, the town is, ironically, located at the junction of Highways 99W and 99E, which now gives true meaning to its name. The first church was established in 1871, the post office opened in 1872, the first jail in 1873, the city hall and fire department in 1873, and the opera house, drug store, hotel, bank and hardware stores in 1890. The annual Scandinavian Festival proudly represents the city's cultural roots.

Moorhead House

Points of Interest

- **Ducky Lee Hotel** (*467 Front*)
  Built as a drugstore then converted to a hotel in 1913.

- **Old City Jail** (*289 4th*)
  Constructed in 1873 at a cost of just over $84. It was once used as a pump house.

- **Pitney House** (*289 4th*)
  Built in 1874. Mary Pitney was born in this home and lived here for 104 years.

- **Fish's Livery Stable** (*5th and Greenwood*)
  Opened about 1913 and was an important stop on the Junction City to Monroe stage run.

- **Blacksmith Shop** (*5th and Greenwood*)
  Located across the street from the livery stable. Opened in 1911.

- **Junction City Electric Railroad Depot** (*5th and Holly*)
  Constructed between 1911 and 1912. The depot saw twenty passenger stops a day and had a 99% on time record. It is now a restaurant with a caboose next door.

- **Founder's Park** (*5th and Holly*)
  Opened in 1904. A Finnish train, used during WWI, is displayed.

- **Junction City Merchandise Store** (*160 6th*)
  Opened in 1890 by W.G. Pickett.

Pitney House

- **Hardware Store** *(170 6th)*
  The store, also built by Pickett, was constructed in 1890.

- **Junction City State Bank** *(180 6th)*
  The bank opened for business in 1890.

- **IOOF Building** *(6th and Greenwood)*
  Across the street from the Mason Building, the Oddfellows Building was constructed in 1909 at a cost of $10,000.

- **Site of Junction City Opera House** *(between 6th and 7th on Front)*
  Reported to be the finest opera house between San Francisco and Portland. Built in 1890, it burned to the ground in 1915.

Danish Lutheran Church

Old City Jail

- **Lee's Drugstore** *(190 6th)*
  Operated by Dr. Lee in 1890.

- **Danish Lutheran Church** *(926 6th)*
  Moved to this site from 7th and Ivy in 1940. Constructed in 1908.

- **G.M. Jackson House** *(670 6th)*
  Jackson, a prominent businessman, built the house in 1910.

- **Mason Building** *(6th and Greenwood)*
  Built in 1909 as a furniture, hardware, stoves and wagon store.

- **City Hall and Fire Department** *(6th and Greenwood)*
  The city offices and fire department were built in 1878.

- **Dr. N.L. Lee House and Museum** *(655 Holly)*
  Built by Junction City's first doctor in 1872. The parlor served as his office.

- **Moorhead House** *(617 Juniper)*
  Built by S.L. Moorhead in 1878. Moorhead was the publisher and founder of the *Junction City Times* newspaper.

- **Washburne Park** *(6th between Maple and Laurel)*
  This is the site of one of Junction City's first schools. The Washburne family donated the land.

- **Cumberland Presbyterian Church** *(7th and Holly)*
  Opened in 1871 and was the first church built in Junction City.

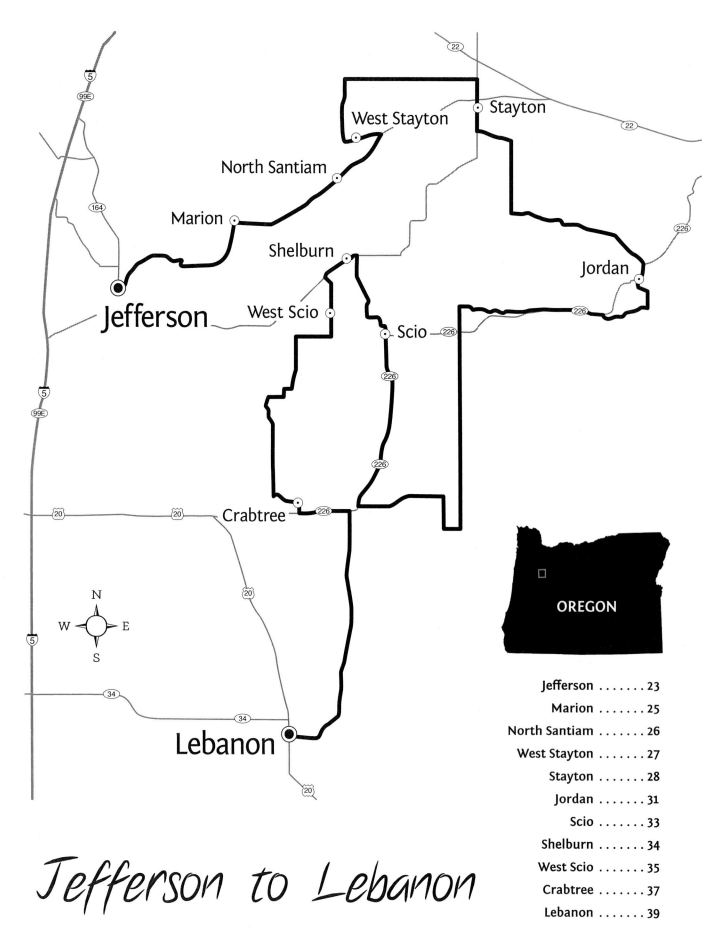

West Stayton

Stayton

North Santiam

Marion

Shelburn

Jordan

West Scio

Scio

Jefferson

Crabtree

Lebanon

OREGON

Jefferson 23

Marion 25

North Santiam 26

West Stayton 27

Stayton 28

Jordan 31

Scio 33

Shelburn 34

West Scio 35

Crabtree 37

Lebanon 39

Jefferson to Lebanon

Covered Bridges and Sacred Cows

Jefferson to Lebanon (67 miles)

Numerous wood covered bridges, old school houses, and century farms dot the landscape along the quiet back roads that meander through fertile farmlands, oak savannas, and evergreen forests in the historic heart of the Willamette Valley and foothills of the Cascade Mountains. This route originates in south Marion County near the community of Jefferson, named after third president Thomas Jefferson, and ends in the north Linn County city of Lebanon, named after the birthplace of Jeremiah Ralston, who had the area surveyed and recorded in 1851.

Points en route include Marion, known for its prize winning cow; the once flourishing railroad communities of Brewster, Whiteaker and Shelburn, the latter built around a curve in the railroad line; and Jordan, named by Circuit Rider Joab Powell who thought he had reached sacred ground. Noteworthy points of interest include the Paris Woolen Mill in Stayton, the Scio museum, located in a railroad caboose, and the Gilkey covered bridge. Start this route at exit 242 on Interstate 5 near the Santiam River, named after the Santiam Indians of the Kalapooia Tribe, who lived here.

countryside near Jefferson

Interstate 5, exit 242 to Jefferson

Distance:
3.3 miles

Directions:
From I-5 exit 242, drive southeast on the Jefferson-Talbot Road toward Jefferson.

Points En Route

(mileage from the stop sign at the I-5 off ramp and Jefferson-Talbot Road intersection)

0.8 miles:
Off to the right in the distance is the Santiam River and site of Hale's Ferry (east of the rest area on Interstate 5). Milton Hale came to the area in 1845 and established the first ferry on the Santiam River. Major flooding in the 1860s destroyed Hale's ferry and landing.

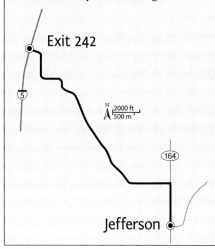

Exit 242

Jefferson

2.3 miles:
Location of the former Mt. Jefferson Woolen Mills. The factory, which closed in 2001, was a small yardage producer. In an average week during its prime, the Jefferson plant processed about 6,000 pounds of wool, the amount sheared from over 11,000 sheep. The Mt. Jefferson Woolen Mills manufactured blankets, men's and women's jackets, and upholstery for airline passenger seats.

2.7 miles:
Jefferson High School.

3.0 miles:
Old farmhouse and barn. At the intersection of Jefferson-Talbot Road and Jefferson Highway, turn right onto Jefferson Highway.

3.1 miles:
Jefferson Middle School.

3.3 miles:
Jefferson.

Jefferson

Elevation: 230 feet

Location:
44.43.088 N • 123.00.568 W

Services:
gas, food

One of the first to explore this part of the Willamette Valley was botanist David Douglas, who discovered and identified many local plants. In 1848, Jacob Conser, early settler and pioneer businessman, came to the Jefferson area. In 1851, he established a ferry on the Santiam River at Ferry and Mill streets and the area became known as Conser's Ferry. The name changed after the Jefferson Institute opened here in 1857. The Jefferson post office opened June 13, 1861 and the town was platted in 1866. The community incorporated in 1870, the same year the railroad reached Jefferson. The first electric lights were installed in 1907. Jefferson, known as the "Frog Jumping Capital of Oregon," is largely a farming community that is experiencing rapid growth. It is home to the annual Mint Harvest Festival and is the self-proclaimed "Mint Capital of the World."

Jefferson United Methodist Church

Points of Interest

- **Santiam River**
  More than one hundred years ago, with constant dredging, the river was navigable for steamships. Once the railroad reached town in 1870, steamboat traffic and dredging ended.

- **Site of Conser's Ferry**
  (Ferry and Mill)
  Boat launching area.

- **Jones Building** *(Main Street)*
  The 1887 building was converted to apartments.

- **Old Meat Market** *(126 N Main)*
  This building housed the butcher shop.

- **Jacob Conser House**
  (128 N Main)
  The 1854 home of the town founder was the first framed structure in Jefferson and now houses the city hall and library. As the Jefferson Hotel, it served as an important stage and pony express stop.

- **Old Houses**
  (173, 212, 230, 234 Mill)
  All are near the ferry landing.

- **Welcome Inn Café**
  (Union and Main)
  This building was erected near the site of the 1857 Jefferson Institute. The institute was legislatively incorporated in 1857, opened in 1876 and closed in 1899.

- **Masonic Lodge**
  (Church and Main)
  The 1899 lodge was constructed as a two-story building, with the lodge upstairs and a theater on the first floor. The 1962 Columbus Day windstorm caused much damage and forced the demolition of the upper floor. The original Lodge was constructed in 1866 near the site of the downtown grocery store.

- **Old House** *(245 N 3rd)*
  Lots of gingerbread.

- **Catholic Church** *(647 N 3rd)*
  Constructed in 1908 and later moved to this location.

Jacob Conser House

- **Cusick Drug Emporium**
  (104 N Main)
  Now the Centre of Main Street Building.

- **Roland Dry Goods** *(107 N Main)*
  Constructed in 1895.

- **Oregon State Bank**
  (109 N Main)
  The former 1895 bank houses the Jefferson Historical Society and museum and serves as the Chamber of Commerce Information Center.

- **Howell Building** *(119 Main)*
  1900.

- **Barber Shop** *(150 Main)*
  Constructed in 1923 and located across the street from the Fire Department. It once housed the local newspaper, *The Jefferson Review*.

- **2nd Oldest House in Jefferson**
  (101 Church)
  Located near the end of Main Street.

- **Jefferson United Methodist Church** *(Church and 2nd)*
  On the National Historic Registry. Built in 1871, and opened as the Methodist-Episcopal Church.

- **Jefferson Highway Bridge**
  (over the Santiam River)
  This is the third bridge to span the river. The 1891 bridge was replaced in 1910. The existing bridge was constructed in 1932.

- **Railroad Bridge**
  (adjacent to the highway bridge)
  The original bridge was built in 1870 and replaced by the current one in 1906.

Jefferson to Marion

Distance:
4.3 miles

Directions:
From Jefferson Elementary School at 2nd and North, drive east on North Avenue toward Marion.

Points En Route

(mileage from the intersection of 2nd and North)

0.1 miles:
Jefferson Cemetery Road. Jefferson Cemetery is 0.4 miles from here. Dates to the 1860s.

1.8 miles:
Old farm and barn.

2.8 miles:
Older home, 4854 Marion Road.

4.3 miles:
Marion

Marion

Elevation: 303 feet

Location:
44.44.965 N • 123.56.018 W

Services:
gas, food

Marion County, Marion Creek and the community of Marion were all named to honor General Francis Marion, Revolutionary War general. A majority of homes and stores are located on the east side of railroad tracks that divide the Marion community into two sections. The old general store is closed and a convenience market now fills the immediate grocery needs of this unincorporated, agricultural community. A world famous Guernsey cow that won three world championships for milk and butter production brought much notoriety to her Marion home. For many years, a monument to this cow stood at the community's entrance.

Former Church

Points of Interest

- **Former Church** (*A Street*)
  Converted to a private residence and more than 100 years old.

- **Marion School** (*B Street*)
  Opened in 1905.

- **Marion City Park**
  (*behind the converted church*)
  Includes a playground and picnic area.

- **Marion Cemetery**
  (*located 0.4 miles up the hill on the west side of the railroad tracks*)
  Grave markers date to 1893.

North Santiam

Elevation: 358 feet

Location:
44.460.040 N • 122.52.716 W

Services:
none

North Santiam is named for its location near the North Santiam River. 1936 is the date displayed on the façade of the old school located across the street from the former general store, now closed and boarded. Diversified farms mostly comprise the small, rural North Santiam area. Other than the school, store, and former gas station, a few homes are the only remaining structures in this community.

old school

Marion to North Santiam

Distance:
3.3 miles

Directions:
From the store at the intersection of Marion Road and Stayton Road, drive east on Stayton Road.

Points En Route

(mileage from the intersection of Stayton Road and Marion Road)

0.6 miles:
Old farm and barn.

1.6 miles:
Marion Church of God Seventh Day Adventist.

3.3 miles:
North Santiam

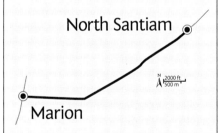

Points of Interest

- **Old School** *(Santiam Loop Road)*
  This 1936 building replaced the original school.

- **Abandoned Gas Station**
  (8910 Stayton Road)
  Concrete pad with pump stations still visible.

- **Santiam General Store**
  (8938 Stayton Road)
  Closed and in need of paint.

North Santiam to West Stayton

Distance:
3.2 miles

Directions:
At the intersection of Stayton Road and Santiam Road Loop, drive northwest on Stayton Road.

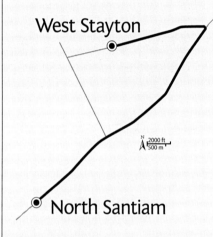

Points En Route

(mileage from the Stayton Road and Santiam Road Loop intersection)

0.6 miles:
Miniature horses.

1.9 miles:
Turn left onto West Stayton Road.

2.3 miles:
Former Bean Alley store (12271 West Stayton Road), named for pole beans farmed nearby. Travel 1/2 mile on Bean Alley to see the "picker shacks" that remain from the 1950s and 1960s.

2.7 miles:
Aged, two-story home.

3.2 miles:
West Stayton

West Stayton

Elevation: 382 feet

Location:
44.47.001 N • 122.52.508 W

Services:
none

West Stayton was established in the 1880s at the same time the narrow gauge Oregon Railway track was laid through fertile farmlands here, instantly making the small community an important shipping terminus. Residents submitted the name Ale for their community after finding an "old ale bottle" near the railroad tracks in 1888. The Ale post office, which operated from 1888 to 1902, was housed in the train depot. It reopened in 1911 under the name West Stayton and closed in 1953. The old West Stayton School sits in the heart of the small community, surrounded by homes, a grain elevator and farms.

Points of Interest

- **West Stayton School**
  The 1911, former grade school is now an alternative educational facility.

miniature horses along road to West Stayton

Bean Alley picker shacks

Stayton

Elevation: 449 feet

Location:
44.48.571 N • 122.48.828 W

Services:
gas, food, B&B, lodging

Located at the confluence of the Santiam Canyon and the Willamette Valley, Stayton is chiefly a farming community only fourteen miles from the state capitol in Salem. Entrepreneurs were attracted to the area by the availability of plentiful, affordable water to generate power. Early water-powered mills included a flourmill, excelsior mill, a cabinet factory and a sash and door factory. Drury S. Stayton, a Baptist minister, farmer, and justice of the peace, built a sawmill here in 1870. The town was platted in 1872, incorporated in 1884 and chartered in 1891. The Paris Woolen Mills, the largest employer in Stayton for more than 100 years, closed in 1989. Efforts to restore the building failed and it was razed in 2003. As it transitioned to more of an agricultural community in the early 20th century, Stayton became known as the "bean capital" of the Willamette Valley. The Stayton Canning Co. Cooperative, now known as Norpac Foods, Inc., was established in about 1924, and remains the largest single employer in Stayton.

W.B. Hobson General Merchandise Store

West Stayton to Stayton

Distance:
4.1 miles

Directions:
Drive east on West Stayton Road.

Points En Route

(mileage from the schoolhouse)

1.4 miles:
Turn right onto Shaff Road.

1.7 miles:
Crossing railroad tracks.

2.7 miles:
Well-maintained, old farmhouse.

4.1 miles:
Stayton

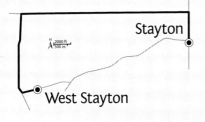

Points of Interest

- **Charles Brown House**
  (1st and E. High)
  In 1902, Brown, a skilled carpenter, designed and built his home next to the Salem Ditch. It was one of the first homes in Stayton with indoor plumbing, electrical wiring, radiant heating and hot water. It served as Stayton's Hospital from 1929 until 1938.

- **D.S. Stayton House**
  (125 E. High)
  The oldest building in Stayton, built in 1872 by the town founder.

- **Carquest Auto Parts**
  (2nd and Water)
  This location was the center of Stayton's early business district.

Charles Brown House

Stayton

Points of Interest (continued)

- **W.H. Hobson General Merchandise Store** *(2nd and Water)*
  Opened in 1882 and was Stayton's first false-front structure.

- **Leander Brown House** *(227 2nd)*
  Constructed in 1885. Brown was Stayton's first Mayor and operated sawmills in Stayton and Mill City.

- **Santiam Historical Society** *(260 2nd)*
  Single story dwelling.

- **Stayton Women's Community Clubhouse** *(260 3rd)*
  Opened in 1928.

- **Old Residence** *(308 E Water)*
  A private residence built on the site of the early, water-powered, rawhide bottom chair factory.

- **Stayton Bank Building** *(311 3rd)*
  Constructed in 1904 and now used by City of Stayton officials.

- **Roy Block** *(349 3rd)*
  Constructed in 1908 and now used as an art gallery.

- **Stayton Automobile Agency** *(429 3rd)*
  Floyd Robertson opened the show room and repair shop in 1910. Motion pictures were shown in this building before the theater opened.

- **W.H. Thomas House** *(622 3rd)*
  A 1908 craftsman. Thomas was the local undertaker.

- **A.D. Gardner House B&B** *(653 3rd)*
  Built in 1898. Gardner was a pharmacist in the 1870s and 1880s. In 1891, he purchased a flourmill that he operated for more than forty years. In his lifetime, he served the community in many leadership capacities, including postmaster for a number of years.

A.D. Gardner House B&B

- **Fred Albus House** *(676 3rd)*
  The 1938 home belonged to the drug store owner.

- **Dr. Charles Brewer House** *(717 3rd)*
  This elegant home belonged to one of Stayton's first doctors. The 1907 structure was office and living quarters for the doctor and his family. It was converted to a Bed and Breakfast in 1986.

- **Odd Fellows Lodge** *(122 3rd)*
  Built in 1912. Lodge meetings were held upstairs and Chevrolets were sold downstairs.

- **Mathieu and Sestak Building** *(239 3rd)*
  This 1935 building replaced the one destroyed by fire in 1934. Mathieu ran a saloon and cigar store. Mathieu was son of Francis X. Mathieu, a Hudson's Bay Trapper.

- **W.E. Thomas Store** *(383 3rd)*
  The local YMCA opened in 1910 as a general merchandise store.

- **Beauchamp Drug Store** *(391 3rd)*
  Opened in 1913, complete with a second floor ballroom.

- **Fire Department** *(400 3rd)*
  The 1936 clay tile and stucco building replaced the original 1895 town hall.

- **Charles Stayton House** *(784 3rd)*
  Built in 1905 by A.D. Gardner as a gift to his daughter Ethel and son-in-law Charles, grandson of the town founder. The house is a mini version of the Gardner house in the next block.

- **Deldrich Block** *(3rd and Florence)*
  Opened in 1912 as a hardware store and later remodeled as a Dodge Dealership.

Stayton to Jordan

- **Farmers and Merchants Bank**
  (3rd and Ida)
  The bank opened in 1911.
  Rumours Restaurant has
  expanded to include the old bank,
  the 1913 newspaper office, and the
  1916 grocery store.

- **Paris Woolen Mills Site**
  (4th and Florence)
  The mill, powered by water
  from the hand-dug Salem Ditch,
  manufactured wool products
  through the 1980s. Little remains.

- **Old Houses**
  (576 Marion and 624 Marion)
  Both are near the park.

- **Pioneer Park** *(7th and Marion)*
  Home to the Stayton-Jordan
  Covered Bridge replica. The
  park opened in 1894. The 1937
  Jordan Bridge was taken apart
  and brought to this site. It was
  destroyed by fire in 1994 and
  rebuilt shortly after. Wilderness
  Park, a 55-acre natural area for
  hiking and bird watching, is
  located across the bridge.

Distance:
9.2 miles

Directions:
At the intersection of 1st and
Water, drive south on First,
which is also called Stayton-
Scio Road.

Points En Route

(mileage from 1st and Water)

0.2 miles:
Santiam River.

0.5 miles:
Turn left on Kingston-Jordan
Highway.

1.5 miles:
Site of Kingston, named to
honor Samuel King, longtime
resident. Not much remains of
"King's town" and the Southern
Pacific Railroad terminus.

1.9 miles:
Grand old home.

2.5 miles:
Queener Cemetery. Dates to
the 1870s.

3.6 miles:
A large home overlooks the
valley.

3.9 miles:
Mt. Pleasant pond with an old
water wheel.

5.0 miles:
The 1854 Mt. Pleasant Church.

5.5 miles:
The 1878 Mt. Pleasant School.
The building is on private
property.

7.8 miles:
At the "Y", stay right.

8.3 miles:
Turn left on Jordan Road.

9.2 miles:
Jordan

*Stayton–Jordan
Covered Bridge*

Jordan

Elevation: 531 feet

Location:
44.43.972 N • 122.41.542 W

Services:
none

Situated high on a hill overlooking the Jordan River Valley, the community was named by circuit rider Joab Powell, who thought he had reached the sacred land of Jordan. The Jordan post office opened in 1874 and closed in 1905. This unincorporated community was once the site of the Monastery of Our Lady of Jordan, a Trappist monastery founded in 1904 and lasting about six years. Nearby, the Jordan River flows into Thomas Creek, making it one of the few rivers that empty into a creek. Several covered bridges span Thomas Creek near here.

Points of Interest

- **Lourdes Catholic Church**
  (top of the hill)
  The parish center is next to the church.

- **Our Lady of Lourdes Cemetery** *(behind the Church)*
  Graves date to the 1880s.

- **Lourdes School**
  (next to the church)
  Beautiful views of valley. The 1898 Bender School, moved to this site, was replaced by this 1960 school building.

Jordan to Scio

Distance:
20.3 miles

Directions:
At the intersection of Jordan Road and Camp Morrison Drive, go right, heading west on Camp Morrison Drive.

Points En Route

(mileage from intersection of Jordan Road and Camp Morrison Drive)

0.6 miles:
1857 Bilyeu-Den Cemetery.

1.3 miles:
The 1936 Hannah Covered Bridge spans Thomas Creek.

1.4 miles:
Intersection with Highway 26. Turn left toward Scio. The old general store is located at the corner. Note the vintage gas pump.

3.6 miles:
Turn right onto Shimanek Bridge Drive. This road will follow Thomas Creek.

5.5 miles:
Turn left onto Richardson Gap Road.

5.5 miles:
Shimanek Covered Bridge. The bridge, constructed in 1966, is one of the few covered bridges painted red in Oregon.

5.6 miles:
Beautiful, well-maintained home with many vintage farm implements.

6.2 miles:
Intersection with Highway 226. Cross the highway, continue on Richardson Gap Road.

8.3 miles:
Mt. Valley Farms.

Lourdes Catholic Church

8.9 miles:
Optional side road to Larwood Covered Bridge.

9.1 miles:
37093 Richardson Gap Road. Tolsoj Lodge #224, ZCBJ Richardson Gap.

9.4 miles:
Site of Richardson Gap Covered Bridge, removed in the 1990s.

10.6 miles:
At the intersection of Richardson Gap Road and Fish Hatchery Road, continue straight on Richardson Gap.

11.6 miles:
1855 Providence Church and Cemetery. Circuit Rider Joab Powell is buried in front of the church building near the road.

11.7 miles:
Turn right onto Griggs Road.

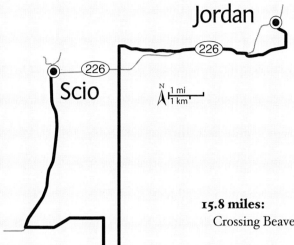

12.2 miles:
At the intersection of Griggs Road and Providence School Road, turn right on Providence School Road.

13.1 miles:
Turn left on Fish Hatchery Road.

15.6 miles:
Intersection with Highway 226. Turn right on Highway 226.

15.8 miles:
Crossing Beaver Creek.

17.2 miles:
Crabtree Creek.

18.8 miles:
Franklin Butte Masonic Cemetery, 1859.

20.1 miles:
House constructed in 1913.

20.3 miles:
Scio

Hannah Covered Bridge

Tolstoj Lodge

Scio

Elevation: 305 feet

Location:
44.42.289 N • 122.50.860 W

Services:
gas, food

After pioneers arrived in 1844, Henry Turner and William McKinley constructed a flourmill on the banks of Thomas Creek. Homes and other businesses soon sprang up around the mill. The mill owners suggested the name Scio after their native home in Ohio. Scio is an anglicized version of *Chios*, an island near Turkey. The Scio post office was established in 1860, and Scio was incorporated in 1866, making it the tenth oldest city in Oregon. Scio is at the heart of an area where five covered bridges span Thomas Creek and Crabtree Creek. Thomas Creek, which flows through the city, was named for Frederick Thomas, who obtained a donation land claim and settled on the banks of the creek in 1846. Mint, hazelnuts, sheep, dairy and beef cattle, and fruits and vegetables are chief agricultural commodities. The Lamb and Wool Fair is a yearly attraction.

ZCBJ–WFLA Hall

Points of Interest

- **Scio Veterans Memorial Park** (*Main and 1st*)
  A cannon is displayed in this park situated on the creek.

downtown storefront

- **Chapin Park and Depot Museum** (*1st and Ash*)
  The museum, open seasonally, is housed in the original West Scio Depot. The depot was dismantled in 1985, then moved and completely rebuilt on the present site, which is bordered by Thomas Creek. A vintage caboose is displayed next to the depot.

- **Downtown Scio** (*1st and Main*)
  False front buildings line Main Street.

- **ZCBJ-WFLA Hall** (*38704 Main next to Thomas Creek*)
  The Zapandai Czechoslovakia Brakasta Jenota building #226 was constructed in 1922 by a Czech fraternal association, reflecting the area's Czechoslovakian influence.

- **Joseph Wesly House** (*38791 Main*)
  Joseph built his house next door to his brother's house.

- **Charles Wesly House** (*38795 Main*)
  Constructed in the latter 1800s.

- **Munkers House** (*38882 Main*)
  Historic home built in the late 1800s.

- **Prill House** (*38945 3rd*)
  A large, Victorian home built in the same era.

- **Franklin Butte Cemetery** (*one mile south of Scio*)
  Dates to 1859.

- **Franklin Butte** (*southeast of town*)
  The highest point in the Scio area.

Scio to Shelburn

Distance:
  2.9 miles

Directions:
  From the intersection of
  NW 1st and N Main, go north
  on N Main.

Points En Route

*(mileage from the intersection of NW
1st and N Main)*

0.2 miles:
  Turn left on 4th (the Jefferson-
  Scio Road) toward Shelburn.

0.9 miles:
  Turn right and travel north on
  Old Miller Cemetery Road.

2.1 miles:
  Miller Pioneer Cemetery, dates
  to 1860.

2.6 miles:
  Turn left on Shelburn Drive.

2.7 miles:
  Old Shelburn School.

2.9 miles:
  Shelburn

Shelburn

Elevation: 354 feet

Location:
44.444.160 N • 122.52.216 W

Services:
none

Sisters Rosa and Mary Miller combined the names of two early area settlers, Shelton and Washburn, to form the name of this community. Shelburn, built along the S-turn in the highway as it crosses the 1887 Southern Pacific railroad tracks, was formed in 1890. A cemetery, on the hill above town, had its first burial, due to a cholera epidemic, in the 1850s. Sawmills once dotted the area. A large hotel was built and operated by Stanley Strylewicz. JR Moses constructed and operated the barbershop. The school, dancehall and a blacksmith shop were focal points in this small town. An old steam engine water tower stands sentinel on private property adjacent to tracks near the site of the old depot.

Railroad Water Tower

Points of Interest

- **Railroad Water Tower**
  A short walk down the tracks.

- **Sucker Creek**
  (near the entrance to town)
  Named for the bottom fish that
  inhabit the stream.

- **Shelburn School**
  Opened in 1912. Now a private
  residence.

Shelburn School

Shelburn to West Scio

Distance:
2.1 miles

Directions:
From the railroad tracks, proceed southwest on Shelburn Drive toward Gilkey.

Points En Route

(mileage from the railroad tracks)

0.9 miles:
Turn left on West Scio Road.

2.1 miles:
West Scio

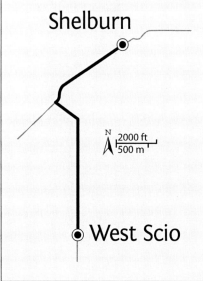

West Scio

Elevation: 320 feet

Location:
44.42.682 N • 122.52.874 W

Services:
food

The name of the community comes from its location west of Scio. The two communities share the same city government, post office, and school system. An old mill is evidence of the area's past timber industry.

Points of Interest

- **Mill** *(near the railroad tracks)*
  Now a graveyard for cars.

- **Victorian House**
  (near the entrance to the mill)
  This house is reputed to be the home of the mill superintendent.

Mill in West Scio

Victorian House

West Scio to Crabtree

Distance:
6.8 miles

Directions:
At the intersection of West Scio Road and Jefferson-Scio Road, travel south on West Scio Road.

Points En Route

(mileage from the intersection of West Scio Road and Jefferson-Scio Road)

0.5 miles:
Turn right and travel west on Robinson Road.

1.5 miles:
Turn left and travel south on Goar Road.

2.6 miles:
Gilkey Covered Bridge. The bridge over Thomas Creek was built in 1939.

2.9 miles:
Gilkey. A historical marker is located at the intersection of Goar Road and Gilkey Road. Gilkey was named after pioneer settlers Allen and William Gilkey, who donated property on which the nearby bridge was built. The brothers were instrumental is bringing the railroad to Scio. The train depot and grain warehouses have been torn down.

3.9 miles:
Go left on Gilkey Road.

4.5 miles:
Riverview School.

5.0 miles:
Victorian house.

6.7 miles:
Turn left on Crabtree Road.

6.8 miles:
Crabtree

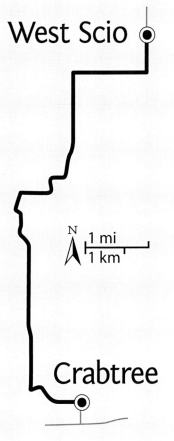

Gilkey Covered Bridge

Crabtree

Elevation: 279 feet

Location:
44.38.115 N • 122.54.121 W

Services:
food

Both the rail station and community were named for D. Fletcher Crabtree when the Southern Pacific Railroad came here. Crabtree Creek and Crabtree Lake were named for Fletcher Crabtree's older brother and Virginia native, pioneer John J. Crabtree, who arrived in the Oregon Country in 1845. Although Crabtree is an unincorporated community, it has a post office with a zip code. The post office and tavern are the only open businesses. At it's peak, Crabtree had two grocery stores, a city hall and a schoolhouse.

General Store

Points of Interest

- **Crabtree Christian Church**
  (37650 Crabtree Road)
  Services are still held in this 1909 building.

- **Crabtree Tavern**
  (37627 Crabtree Road)
  Formerly a hardware and mercantile store.

- **General Store**
  (37585 Crabtree Road)
  The old store and meat market opened in 1909. Frozen food lockers are still visible through the windows.

- **Old House** *(37575 Crabtree Road)*
  A large home on the main street of town.

- **Crabtree Community Center**
  (37524 Crabtree Road)
  Constructed in the 1920s.

- **Former Crabtree School**
  (37425 Crabtree Road)
  1918.

- **Hoffman Covered Bridge**
  (1.6 miles on Hungry Hill Road)
  Built in 1936. The bridge has a ninety-foot span and was named for the builder.

Crabtree Christian Church

Crabtree to Lebanon

Distance:

7.7 miles

Directions:

At the intersection of Hungry Hill Road and Crabtree Road, go left, traveling south on Crabtree Road.

Points En Route

(mileage from the intersection of Hungry Hill Road and Crabtree Road)

0.6 miles:

Turn left on Highway 226, the Albany-Lyons Road.

1.2 miles:

House with a water tower.

1.5 miles:

Turn right on Brewster Road.

3.3 miles:

Griggs School, built in 1922. Old playground equipment is visible behind the former school building, now a private home. Behind the school, on Bond Road, are millponds and the concrete foundation of an old lumber mill.

4.6 miles:

Site of Brewster, located at the corner of Brewster Road and Shady Oak Lane. Settler Alexander Brewster began farming here in the 1860s. It was an important grain shipping point on the Southern Pacific Railroad. The depot was dismantled in the 1950s.

5.1 miles:

Lacomb Road. This road leads to Lacomb, a small community settled by J.E. Turnidge. Turnidge suggested the name of Tacoma for his settlement, which was rejected by postal authorities. The Lacomb Cemetery, located on Ford Mill Road, dates to the 1890s. The Lacomb Grocery Store was built about 1925. A blacksmith shop operated next door to the store. Across from the store was a restaurant and roller rink, both constructed in the 1930s. The old Lacomb Baptist Church is located at 34400 Meridian Road. On September 22, 2007, a local couple claims to have seen UFOs over the Lacomb General Store.

6.4 miles:

An old weather vane.

7.4 miles:

Site of Whiteaker. Named after Oregon's first governor. The Whiteaker post office opened in 1880 and closed in 1903. Beaver were trapped in the creeks around the community. A general store was located in near the tracks.

7.7 miles:

Lebanon

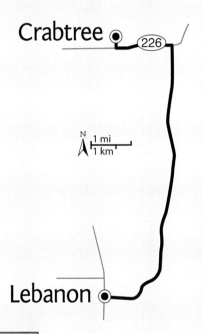

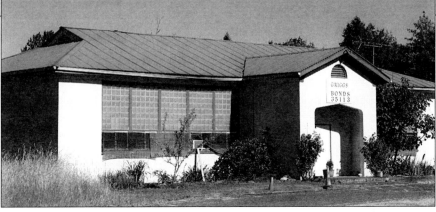

Griggs School

Lebanon

Elevation: 351 feet

Location:
44.32.259 N • 122.54.258 W

Services:
gas, food, lodging

Lebanon was originally known as Peterson's Gap, named after Asa Peterson who settled here in the 1840s. It was also called Kees Station and Kees Precinct, named after 1848 settlers Jacob and Morgan Kees. Jeremiah Ralston surveyed the community in 1851, renaming the community Lebanon after his home in Tennessee. The Lebanon post office opened the same year. A different post office opened in 1851 under the name of Santyam. That name was changed to Washington Butte in 1852 and joined with the Lebanon post office in 1855. The town incorporated in 1878. The railroad came to Lebanon in 1880. The newspaper, the Lebanon Express, published its first paper in 1887. Electricity came to town in 1889 and the first telephones were connected in 1890. The Lebanon Canal was hand dug in 1891 and 1892. The first paper mill operated in 1891. The railroad bridge over the Santiam River was constructed in 1910. Lebanon was a territorial stage stop along the Cascade Wagon Road. Lebanon boasts thirty-eight sites on the Linn County Historical Registry and seven listed on the National Historical Registry. Until 2005, Lebanon was home to one of the last drive-in movie theaters in the state. It was demolished to make room for a Super Wal-Mart despite protests by preservationists. Lebanon was once home of the world's largest plywood mill and is known as an important strawberry producer. The annual Strawberry Festival has been held here since 1909 and boasts "The World's Largest Strawberry Shortcake."

Scroggin Feed and Seed

Points of Interest

- **Lebanon City Library** *(626 2nd)*
  Opened in 1913 as the Lebanon Hospital.

- **School Park** *(50 3rd)*
  Built on the site of the 1852 school.

- **Lebanon Train Depot** *(735 3rd)*
  Built in 1908, replacing the 1880 depot.

- **Scroggin Feed and Seed**
  (280 W Sherman)
  Originally John Settle's Grain Warehouse, built circa 1870. Ralph Scroggin was a subsequent early owner.

- **Thad Sterling House**
  (310 W Grant)
  Built circa 1896. Sterling was active in the feedstore in the John Settle Grain Warehouse. He sold the house to Ralph Scroggin, around 1910. Ralph, son of J.P. Scroggin, served as Mayor in the late 1930s and owned the Scroggin Feed Mill.

- **Methodist Episcopal Church**
  (90 E Vine)
  Constructed in 1910.

- **Presbyterian Church** *(145 Ash)*
  The church was established 1881 and the building constructed in 1910.

- **J.P. Scroggin House** *(185 W Ash)*
  Circa 1892. Scroggin ran the Seamore and Scroggin Sawmill and, in 1896, opened the bank later known as the Lebanon National Bank.

- **Lebanon Pioneer Cemetery**
  (200 Dodge)
  The cemetery opened in 1850 when a 13-year old girl was buried there.

- **John Baker House**
  (515 E Grant)
  1895. Baker operated a nearby sawmill.

- **Booth House** (*486 Park*)
  The 1906 home of Lebanon's first doctor.

- **Ralston Square Park** (*925 Park*)
  Spans almost 2.5 acres.

- **John Ralston Cottage**
  (*481 Main*)
  Ralston was the son of town founder Jeremiah, who built this home in 1887. Note the leaded glass windows.

- **Gem Theater** (*644 Main*)
  Opened in the 1940s.

- **Lebanon Hotel**
  (*651 and 661 Main*)
  The old hotel was open for business in 1913,

- **Kuhn Theater** (*668 Main*)
  Cap Kuhn owned both the Gem Theater and this theater, which opened in 1936.

- **Courtney Block** (*712 Main*)
  1900 construction.

- **The Garland – Bach Meyer Building** (*748 Main*)
  Built in 1910, this building was

the courthouse until 1918 and from 1919 to 1987, the JC Penney Department Store.

- **Andrews and Hackleman Building** (*780 S Main*)
  The two-story structure opened in 1886. The upstairs served as a Masonic Lodge.

- **First National Bank**
  (*809 S Main*)
  Built in 1910 and now Wells Fargo Bank.

- **Lebanon Creamery Building**
  (*853 S Main*)
  1928 construction.

- **City Hall** (*925 S Main*)
  The 1928 building once faced Maple Street.

- **Louis Crandall House**
  (*959 Main*)
  A 1906 Victorian. Louis and his brother Albert operated the Crandall Brothers Planing Mill that produced high quality furniture and building materials.

- **Elkins Flour Mill**
  (*Olive and Eaton*)
  This large, three-story flourmill was built between 1871 and 1878. It was constructed without any nails and is located behind Linn-Benton Community College offices.

- **Masonic and IOOF Cemeteries** (*off highway 20 near the north entrance to town*)
  Dramatic tombstones of many of Lebanon's early settlers.

- **Booth Park** (*Grant and Hiatt*)
  A large park with restrooms, playground, and picnic area.

- **River Park**
  (*Grant and Brewster Road*)
  Boat launch, picnic, restrooms, and fishing.

Elkins Flour Mill

John Ralston Cottage

40

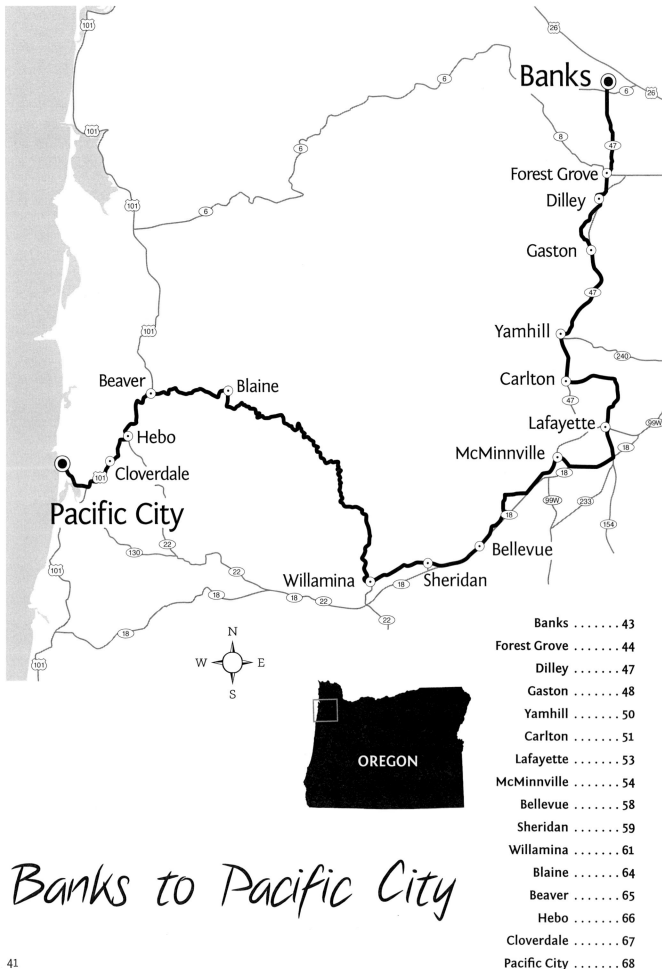

Banks

Forest Grove
Dilley

Gaston

Yamhill

Carlton

Lafayette

McMinnville

Bellevue

Beaver   Blaine

Hebo

Cloverdale

Pacific City

Willamina   Sheridan

OREGON

N
W   E
S

Banks to Pacific City

Banks 43
Forest Grove 44
Dilley 47
Gaston 48
Yamhill 50
Carlton 51
Lafayette 53
McMinnville 54
Bellevue 58
Sheridan 59
Willamina 61
Blaine 64
Beaver 65
Hebo 66
Cloverdale 67
Pacific City 68

City Lights, Country Sites, Mountain Views, Ocean Blues

Banks to Pacific City (92 miles)

This route begins twenty-four miles west of Portland, just outside the Urban Growth boundary, in the small, rural, Washington County community of Banks and ends at Pacific City via the Willamette Valley and Coast Range Mountains. Paved roads wind through old growth timber, fertile farmlands, and swift mountain streams.

Habitats vary dramatically en route from city to country, valley to second-growth timber, and from wetlands to the marine mix of estuaries, dunes and beaches. On this tour you will discover Oregon's oldest college, climb on huge erratic rocks deposited over 10,000 years ago by immense icebergs, experience Yamhill County wine country, pass by some of the best steelhead waters in the state, and watch dory boats launched in the Pacific surf.

Christmas Tree farm near Bellevue

Banks

Elevation: 250 feet

Location:
45.36.517 N • 123.06.383 W

Services:
gas, food, lodging, B&B

Banks Log Cabin

The first known people in the area were the Atfalatis Indians, who roamed here hundreds of years before pioneers settled in the North-west. Hudson Bay trappers constructed a dairy in the area, decades before Virginia born Peyton Wilkes established his 1847 land claim in what is now Banks. By the 1860s, a small community had formed. William Mills donated land for the cemetery in 1870, today known as the Union Point Cemetery, where Peyton and Anna Wilkes are buried. Originally known as Wilkes, the post office opened in 1902 under the name of Banks, to compliment Robert and John Banks, early settlers. The first name chosen for the post office was Turner, but a community in Marion County already claimed that name. The first church was built in 1908 and the first bank in 1909. In 1910, about 100 Japanese families came here to farm, specializing in strawberry crops. Banks incorporated in 1921, constructed a reservoir for its water supply in 1924, and added the sewer system in 1938. *Star Wars: The Empire Strikes Back* was filmed here in 1980. The Spirit of Oregon dinner train winds into the Coast Range Mountains from the nearby town of Roy. Agriculture and the timber industry remain important to the economy of the Banks area with many farms, dairies and livestock operations located here. Banks touts itself as the "best of both worlds" where residents both enjoy a relaxed, country lifestyle and take advantage of short commutes to jobs in the Portland metropolitan area.

Points of Interest

- **Former Train Depot**
  (162 Commerce)
  The sign above the entrance reads, "Port of Tillamook Bay RR." It is now part of the Banks Lumber Company.

- **Banks United Methodist Church** *(131 Depot)*
  Opened in 1908 with stained glass windows.

- **Banks City Hall**
  (100-120 N Main)
  An old brick building.

- **Banks General Store**
  (130 N Main)
  Circa 1905.

- **Banks Hardware** *(150 N Main)*
  The hardware store, complete with its original floors, was built in 1902 and is still in business today.

- **Banks Log Cabin** *(290 S Main)*
  The cabin was built for Boy Scout Troop 240 in 1930.

- **House** *(291 S Main)*
  Across from the log cabin, this is one of Banks' finest.

- **Sunset Park** *(S Main)*
  Baseball fields, picnicking.

- **West Fork of Dairy Creek**
  (Cedar Canyon Road)
  This is the area that Peyton Wilkes settled in 1847. The name comes from Hudson Bay Company employees who operated a dairy in this vicinity before the Wilkes came to the area.

Banks to Forest Grove

Distance:
5.5 miles

Directions:
From the intersection of Main and Sunset at the Log Cabin, drive south toward Forest Grove.

Points En Route

(mileage from the Boy Scout Log Cabin at Main and Sunset)

0.7 miles:
Grand, old home.

1.7 miles:
To visit Tualatin Estate Vineyards, turn right on Greenville Road.

2.1 miles:
Century Farm.

3.7 miles:
Sunset Grove Golf Course.

4.8 miles:
David Hill Winery is four miles to the right on Purdin Road.

5.5 miles:
Forest Grove
(turn right at the light)

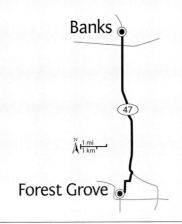

Forest Grove

Elevation: 210 feet

Location:
45.31.173 N • 123.06.319 W

Services:
gas, food, lodging, B&B

Kalapuya Indians were the first known people in the Forest Grove area. The first settlers, Alvin and Abigail Smith, built a log cabin home in 1841. Harvey Clark arrived in 1845 and helped start the Congregational Church. In 1849, Harvey Clark and Tabitha Brown established the Tualatin Academy, a school for children of settlers, which later became Pacific University. The name Forest Grove was officially recognized in 1859. 100-ton steam ships navigated the Tualatin River to Forest Grove in 1869 and docked at Emerick's Landing. The first newspaper, *The Forest Grove Independent*, was established in 1872, the same year the city was officially incorporated. Electric power first came in 1892. In 1893 a city ordinance was passed requiring brick construction of all buildings in the downtown core area, a reaction to the terrible fire that destroyed most of the wooden buildings. The first telephones were installed in 1894. By 1909, electric streetcars connected Forest Grove with Portland and McMinnville. 1909 was also the year the public library opened. The Tualatin Academy officially became Pacific University in 1914. Experience 150 years of architectural history and more than 100 homes and buildings via the walking tour of historic Old Town and The Clark District. Maps are available at the Chamber of Commerce. There are over a dozen wineries just minutes from downtown offering tasting rooms, fine food, music and art events, gift shops and tours. Every September, four tons of locally grown fresh corn is consumed at the Annual Corn Roast held on the grounds of Pacific University. Thousands of visitors enjoy the annual summer Concours d'Elegance, one of four premier vintage car shows in the United States.

Masonic Grand Lodge

Points of Interest

- **Alvin T. Smith House** *(1504 Elm)*
  Built by the town founder in 1856, it is the oldest home in Forest Grove.

- **Historical Marker** *(near the tree at the corner of Elm and 15th)*
  Marks the site where Pacific University was founded.

Forest Grove

Points of Interest (continued)

- **Grove Theater** (*2028 Pacific*)
  Opened in the 1920s.

- **Clark National Historic District Walking Tour**
  (*begin at 2417 Pacific*)
  More than 100 businesses and homes are identified on a walking tour of old Forest Grove.

- **Masonic Grand Lodge**
  (*3505 Pacific*)
  Built as a retirement center for Masons, the 1922 structure is now the McMenamin's Grand Lodge Hotel and Restaurant.

- **Marsh House** (*2218 College Way*)
  Built in 1879 to be the home of Dr. Marsh, who died before it was completed.

- **Blank House** (*217 A*)
  In 1858, it also served as the Stage Coach stop.

- **Harry Crosley House** (*2125 A*)
  Constructed in 1895.

- **LaTourette House** (*2314 A*)
  1873.

- **Thomas Hines House**
  (*1604 Birch*)
  Built in 1859 and moved to this site in 1888.

- **Anderson Building #1**
  (*2001-2003 Main*)
  A 1917 clothing store.

- **1st National Bank** (*2004 Main*)
  Opened about 1910.

- **Anderson Building #2**
  (*2007-2011 Main*)
  Same owner as 2001 Main. Former home of the Holbrook Lodge (Masons) and the Star Theater.

- **Haines/Bailey Building**
  (*2008 Main*)
  Constructed in 1890.

- **Nixon Building** (*2012-2016 Main*)
  A dentist office in 1912.

- **Paterson Building**
  (*2013-2017 Main*)
  Originally a 1926 bakery, later furniture store.

- **Holbrook Lodge #30**
  (*2019 Main*)
  This Masonic Lodge was chartered in 1860.

- **Caples and Thomas Building**
  (*2020 Main*)
  An 1893 general merchandise store.

- **Buxton and Roe Building**
  (*2030 Main*)
  Home to the undertaker and a hardware store.

- **Ingles and Porter Building**
  (*2036 Main*)
  A jewelry store and a shoe store in 1892.

Occur Bowen House

- **Pacific University Museum**
  (*Old College Hall, 2021 Council*)
  The museum is housed in the original 1850 Tualatin Academy building.

- **Sidney Marsh House**
  (*2216 College Way*)
  Built in 1856.

- **Forest Grove Grange #202**
  (*1917 B*)
  Late 1900s.

- **Jerome Porter House** (*2119 B*)
  This home was constructed in 1873.

- **Occur Bowen House** (*2325 B*)
  This home was built in 1895.

Pacific University Museum

- **Wagner Building** *(2038 Main)* 1892 drugstore and doctor office.

- **Keep Building** *(2042 Main)* The office of Dr. Via in 1892.

- **Lincoln Park** *(2725 Main)* The oldest of Forest Grove's parks. Swimming pool, ball fields, picnic area, and restrooms.

- **A.C. Brown House** *(Sunset Drive near Willamina Ave)* About 1863.

- **Lila Smith House** *(2011 Hawthorne)* Constructed in 1865.

- **Patton/Nixon House** *(2018 Hawthorne)* 1865 construction.

- **S. Hughes House** *(2111 Hawthorne)* Built about 1865.

- **A.I. Macrum House** *(2225 12th)* This lovely 1888 home with period décor is called "The Castle." The house served as a hospital during WWI.

- **J.E. Bailey House** *(2422 15th)* Constructed in 1892.

- **William Perry House** *(2434 15th)* 1905.

- **Thomas Roe House** *(2126 17th)* The 1872 home of businessman Roe.

- **Joseph Gale Park** *(3014 18th)* Named for an early settler.

- **Train Station** *(1936 19th)* Circa 1920.

- **B. Cornelius House** *(2314 19th)* The founder of Cornelius built this home in 1875.

- **Robb-Roberts House** *(2606 17th)* Constructed in 1875.

- **Dr. Bishop House** *(1806 22nd)* Circa 1862.

- **M.E. Dilley House** *(1933 22nd)* This is the 1870 home of the founder of Dilley.

Forest Grove to Dilley

Distance:
2.1 miles

Directions:
From the intersection of Pacific Avenue and B Street, drive south on B Street toward Gaston and McMinnville.

Points En Route

(mileage from the intersection of Pacific and B)

0.6 miles:
Gales Creek.

1.0 miles:
Turn right on Highway 47.

1.4 miles:
Turn right on Hiatt Road.

1.7 miles:
L Bar T Bison Ranch.

1.9 miles:
Turn left on Dilley Road.

2.1 miles:
Montinore Winery (3663 SW Dilley Road).

2.1 miles:
Dilley

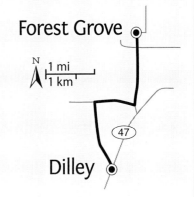

Dilley

Elevation: 250 feet

Location:
45.29.261 N • 123.07.358 W

Services:
none

Montinore Winery

Dilley was named for pioneer Milton Dilley, who owned much land here and along Gales Creek. In 1849, Horace and Matilda Parsons were the first permanent settlers to the area. Parsons built a gristmill on the Tualatin River in 1850. The Dilley School District was formed in 1860. A flourmill opened in 1863. The Dilley post office opened in 1873 and closed in 1961. The community was platted in 1874 about the same time that railroad track was laid through town. M. McLeod constructed a sawmill in 1880 and the rail station was built in 1894, twenty years after the track was put down. At its prime, Dilley had two churches, two saloons, a flourmill, gristmill, insurance agent, shoe store, general store, dancehall, sawmill, and a grange hall. In 1967 the highway was rerouted around Dilley and the old store and gas station were torn down.

Points of Interest

- **Dilley Mansion**
  (3663 SW Dilley Road)
  Wrongly called the Dilley Mansion as no members of the Dilley family ever lived in the home. The private residence was built in 1905 for the Forbes family. Forbes was a local attorney.

- **Old House** (3840 SW Dilley Road)
  A wagon wheel and a wrap-around porch.

- **Llama Ranch**
  (3964 SW Dilley Road)
  Near the school.

- **Old House** (4322 SW Dilley Road)
  This neglected home has beautiful stained glass windows.

- **Dilley School**
  (4115 SW Dilley Road)
  The first Dilley school opened in 1862.

- **Dilley Church**
  1906.

Dilley Mansion

Dilley to Gaston

Distance:
4.4 miles

Directions:
At the intersection of Dudney and Highway 47, drive south on Highway 47 toward Gaston.

Points En Route

(mileage from the intersection of Dudney and Highway 47)

0.3 miles:
Turn right on Old Highway 47.

1.3 miles:
Mt. Olive Cemetery, which dates to 1902.

1.4 miles:
Plum Hill Vineyards.

2.0 miles:
Stately farmhouse.

2.5 miles:
Old Highway 47 and Scoggin Valley Road intersect. Continue on Old Highway 47 as it crosses SW Scoggin Valley Road. Cross the railroad tracks.

2.7 miles:
Patton Valley water tower. Near the tower is the intersection of Old Highway 47 and Patton Valley.

3.2 miles:
Patton Valley Vineyards.

3.3 miles:
Keep left on Old Highway 47.

3.7 miles:
Turn right and stay on Old Highway 47.

4.4 miles:
Gaston

(map showing Dilley, Highway 47, and Gaston with scale 1 mi / 1 km, N arrow)

Gaston

Elevation: 300 feet

Location:
45.43.693 N • 123.14.139 W

Services:
gas, food

The town was named for Joseph Gaston, an 1862 pioneer emigrant from Ohio, who actively promoted the west side railroad that ran from southwest Portland. Gaston helped build the narrow gauge line from Dayton to Yamhill in 1872 and then the line from Yamhill to Sheridan in 1878. Gaston went on to become the president of the Oregon Central Railroad Company. He died at the age of seventy-nine in 1913. The first school in Gaston held classes in 1863, the stage line began operating in 1871, and the post office opened in 1873.

Points of Interest

- **Gaston City Hall** *(116 Front)*
  Replaced the original structure.

- **Knights of the Pythias #104** *(212 Front)*
  Dates to the 1920s.

- **Gaston Community Church** *(202 2nd)*
  This church was built in 1924.

- **Gaston Congregational Church** *(209 2nd)*
  One-foot square hand-hewn timbers hold up this 1880s church that has been converted into a residence. The stained glass windows, hand-hewn floors, and the original wood stove remain inside the building.

Gaston Congregational Church

Gaston

Points of Interest (continued)

- **Joseph Gaston House**
  (300 Park)
  Originally the home of the town founder, this house now serves as the local school district office.

- **Gaston Bank** (Front and Park)
  The vault has been removed and the structure remodeled to serve as a tavern. The old, hand-laid floor tiles exhibit intentional pattern errors by workers during construction.

- **Bates House** (102 Oak)
  Built in 1890.

- **Old House** (314 Park)
  Constructed in the 1870s.

- **Mill Street Business Complex**
  (108 Mill)
  This structure was built in 1935.

Joseph Gaston House

Gaston to Yamhill

Distance:
  7.5 miles

Directions:
  At the intersection of Park Avenue and Highway 47, drive south on Highway 47 toward Yamhill.

Points En Route

(mileage from the intersection of Park Avenue and Highway 47)

2.7 miles:
  Site of Wapato. Named after the lake that covers territory in both Yamhill and Washington counties, the town was first referred to as either Lake Wapato or Wapatoo. The Wapato post office was established southeast of Gaston in 1853 and discontinued in 1865. A second Wapato post office opened in 1883 and was discontinued in 1886. Look for the site of the old Wapato School (near the intersection of Highway 47 and Wapato School Road).

4.7 miles:
  Cove Orchard.

4.8 miles:
  Cove Orchard Store. The store, remodeled several times and now closed, is more than 100 years old. The gas pumps were removed in the 1970s. Rough-hewn, exposed lumber is visible in the back of the store.

7.5 miles:
  Yamhill

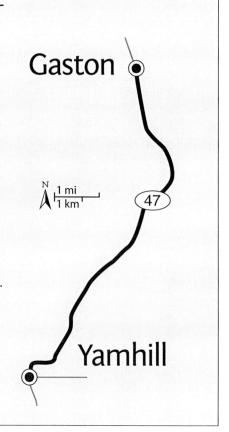

Yamhill

Elevation: 182 feet

Location:
45.20.282 N • 123.11.301 W

Services:
gas, food

While the actual meaning is uncertain, the name "Yamhill" is thought to come from early trappers referring to the Native Americans in the area as the Yamehals, meaning "Those who dwell in houses on the Yellow River." The post office opened in 1851. The buildings in the downtown core area were built by Chinese laborers. The bricks were hand-made by the workers at a factory one-half mile from the town on Pike Road. Old Yamhill used to boast two blacksmith shops, two banks, a Chinese Laundry, and a general store. The town incorporated in 1891. Rings to tie up horses are found embedded in the sidewalk along Main Street. The Yamhill-Carlton AVA is home to wine industry pioneers and includes sixty vineyards, thirty wineries and 1,500 acres of grapes. Once primarily known for tree-fruit orchards, nurseries and livestock, wheat and logging, the area is now known as one of the country's finest producers of cool-climate varietals and award winning wines.

barn near Yamhill

Points of Interest

- **T and E Store** *(110 Main)*
  Built in 1910, the store displays products from the turn of the century. Items are displayed on a walkway twelve feet above the main floor that wraps the entire store.

- **Yamhill United Methodist Church** *(195 S Laurel)*
  Built in 1898.

- **Lee Laughlin House**
  (100 S. Laurel)
  1879 beauty with porch and gingerbread.

- **Beulah City Park** *(E 3rd)*

- **Yamhill Christian Church**
  (265 W Main)
  Built in 1881.

- **Old House** *(320 Main)*
  Across the street from the Christian Church.

- **John Marion Bunn House**
  (285 3rd)
  This home dates to 1860, making it the oldest in town.

- **Old House** *(225 N Olive)*
  Beautiful Victorian.

- **Old House** *(260 N Olive)*
  Lovely two-story.

- **Old House** *(310 N Olive)*
  The last home on the block.

- **Old House** *(225 S Olive)*
  May have been a hotel or boarding house.

- **Johnston and Hutchcraft Store** *(1st and Maple)*
  Their names are embossed in the cement entry of this 1908 building. Fire damaged the second story in 1937.

- **Yamhill Bank** *(120 Maple)*
  1912. Note the tilework near the original entrance.

- **CDEDBD Store** *(185 Maple)*
  Trinkets and coffee are sold in the store that is on the site of the old Yamhill Hotel.

- **Yamhill-Carlton High School**
  (275 N Maple)
  1915.

- **St. John's Catholic Church**
  (445 N Maple)
  Opened in 1903.

- **Fitzgerald Farm**
  (8490 Moore's Valley Road)
  Since 1903.

Distance:
2.8 miles

Directions:
From the blinking light downtown at Maple and Main, drive south on Highway 47.

Points En Route

(mileage from Maple and Main)

0.7 miles:
An old farmhouse getting a facelift.

1.2 miles:
Zimmerman Century Farm.

1.4 miles:
Yamhill Cemetery, established in the 1850s.

2.4 miles:
A once grand farmhouse.

2.8 miles:
Carlton

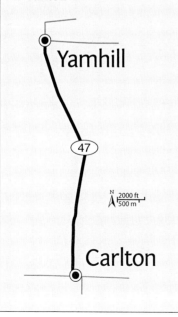

Carlton

Elevation: 198 feet

Location:
45.17.171 N • 123.10.394 W

Services:
gas, food, B&B

Although there is some debate whether the town was named after one-time county commissioner Wilson Carl, Carlton was probably named for John Carl Sr. at the time the Westside railroad established a station in the community about 1874. Carl was an early settler in this area and owned a farm in the prime Yamhill Valley farming area. The Carlton post office was established in 1874 and the town incorporated in 1899. Electricity came to town in 1906 and city water in 1911. A 1921 fire destroyed almost one downtown city block. Today, numerous wineries and tasting rooms occupy much of Main Street and the core downtown area. "Fun Days", an annual event typically held on the 4th Saturday in June, includes many family friendly activities.

Carlton Train Depot

Points of Interest

- **Carlton State Bank** *(105 Main)*
  The 1910 bank building is now a wine tasting room.

- **First Baptist Church**
  (226 Main)
  Built in 1915, it replaced the 1870 building.

- **Upper City Park and Pool**
  (W. Main)
  Swim, picnic and play in the 1921 park.

- **Carlton Community Christian Church** *(500 Main)*
  Constructed in the 1870s.

- **Carlton Theater**
  (on Main, between Pine and Yamhill)
  The first theater burned and this one replaced it in 1945. The old marquis is all that remains.

- **Carlton Train Depot**
  (intersection of Main and Pine)
  In 1928, this depot was moved from its original spot on the other

side of the railroad tracks. The Oregon Central, or the Westside Railroad, first came through town in the 1870s. The restored building now houses Tyrus Evan Winery.

- **Carlton Inn** (*648 Main*)
  A 1921 home converted to a Bed and Breakfast.

- **Zimmerman Grain Elevators** (*Pine and Monroe*)
  The tallest elevator was built in 1916.

- **Old House** (*419 S Park*)
  A two-story with stately columns.

- **Wennerberg Park** (*Cunningham and Grant*)
  Home to the annual "A Walk in the Park" festival, a weekend benefit for local charities that combines artists and musicians with local restaurants and wineries.

- **Carlton Fire Department Building** (*Kutch*)
  The CFD building was built around 1912.

- **R.R. Thompson House** (*517 Kutch*)
  Remodeled into a B & B.

- **Victorian House** (*562 Kutch*)
  Neat gingerbread on this one hundred year-old home.

- **Grace Baptist Church** (*2nd and Monroe*)
  Constructed of locally made brick.

- **Carlton School** (*229 2nd*)
  The 1907 school was remodeled as apartments in 1966.

Zimmerman Grain Elevators

Carlton to Lafayette

Distance:
7.0 miles

Directions:
From the intersection of Main and Pine, travel east on Main toward Lafayette.

Points En Route

(mileage from Main and Pine)

0.4 miles:
Carlo and Julian Winery.

2.1 miles:
Lemelsen Vineyards (Stag Hollow Road).

2.8 miles:
Picturesque farm.

3.7 miles:
Turn right on Abbey Road.

4.7 miles:
Trappist Abbey (9200 NE Abbey Road). Cloistered, Cistercian monks live and work at this 1350-acre monastery founded in Pecos NM and moved here in 1955. The campus includes a retreat center, bindery and bakery.

5.4 miles:
Brookside Inn. (8243 NE Abbey Road).

6.0 miles:
Lobenhaus B & B. 6975 NE Abbey Road.

7.0 miles:
Lafayette

Lafayette

Elevation: 185 feet

Location:
45.14.411 N • 123.06.413 W

Services:
gas, food, B&B

One of the oldest communities in Oregon, Lafayette was founded in 1847 by Joel Perkins and named after Lafayette, Indiana. The post office was established in 1851, incorporated in 1878, and quickly became the Yamhill County seat of government until it was transferred to McMinnville in 1889. Lafayette was once known as the "Athens of the West" for being a great vacation destination as well as site of eloquent oratory from some of the lawyers who served in the territory. Lafayette was also the home of Abigail Scott Duniway of women's suffrage fame. Lafayette has the distinction of hosting the first county fair in Oregon, which occurred on October 7, 1854. Lafayette is the third oldest town in Oregon, ranking behind Astoria and Portland.

Lafayette School House

Points of Interest

- **Lafayette School House**
  (748 Highway 99)
  The 1912 two-story structure is now an antique mall, and its gymnasium is home to truckloads of antique furniture.

- **Historical Marker**
  (corner of 2nd and Adams)
  Marks the location of the 1846 Yamhill County Court, the first in the Oregon Territory.

- **Lafayette Commons Park**
  (2nd between Adams and Monroe)
  Built on the historic grounds of the first Yamhill County Courthouse, the park has restrooms and ball fields.

- **Poling Memorial Church**
  (605 Market)
  Constructed in the 1890s and now the Yamhill County Historical Museum.

- **Miller Museum** *(657 Market)*
  Next to the Historical Museum and built in 1994. There are several gristmill wheels in the front and side yards.

- **Lafayette Park** *(7th and Market)*
  Playground equipment, picnic area, and restrooms.

- **Lafayette Pioneer Cemetery**
  (Duniway Road)
  Take 7th to Duniway. The cemetery is one of the oldest in the state, dating to the 1850s.

- **Alfred P. Fletcher Farmhouse**
  (1007 3rd)

- **James M. and Paul R. Kelty House B&B** *(675 3rd)*
  Built in 1872 by James M. Kelty, an 1852 emigrant on the Oregon Trail. Kelty was a merchant and served as County Sheriff. The house became the country home of his son, Paul R. Kelty, editor of *The Oregonian* newspaper. The Colonial Revival style house, surrounded by 200 year-old native trees, is on the National Historic Register and is now operated as a B&B and wedding venue.

- **Joel Perkins Park**
  (5th and Madison)
  Donated before 1850 as a "public square" by the town founder, Joel Perkins, when he laid out the blocks and town lots. The recently renovated park includes a covered picnic shelter and playground.

- **Yamhill Locks Park**
  (0.5 miles north on Highway 99)
  Picnic under a canopy of ancient Douglas Firs in the 7.1 acre park that was the site of the old ferry landing. Remains of the locks built to allow large boats to navigate the river are visible here.

Lafayette to McMinnville

Distance:
3.5 miles

Directions:
From the intersection of 3rd (Highway 99) and Madison, drive east on Madison (SE Lafayette Highway) toward Highway 18 (SE Dayton Bypass) toward McMinnville.

Points En Route

(mileage from the intersection of 3rd and Madison)

0.2 miles:
Terry Park. A riverfront park with a skateboard area.

0.3 miles:
Crossing the Yamhill River.

0.4 miles:
Old farm with grain elevators.

0.7 miles:
Dairy farm.

1.4 miles:
An old farmhouse that has seen better days.

2.1 miles:
Turn right on Highway 18, traveling south.

3.5 miles:
McMinnville

McMinnville

Elevation: 157 feet

Location:
45.12.402 N • 123.11.511 W

Services:
gas, food, lodging, B&B, RV

W.T. Newby, an early emigrant on the Oregon Trail, came to Oregon in 1843 and settled near the present site of McMinnville in 1844. He named McMinnville after his hometown in Tennessee. In 1853, Newby built a gristmill on his land along Cozine Creek and, soon after, donated land to form the town, including six acres for a school that would eventually become Linfield College. Millstone remains are located in what is today the lower City Park. Newby opened a general store in 1854 and the post office opened in 1855. In 1856, the original town site was platted and by 1866, McMinnville had five stores, three blacksmith shops, two wagon shops, two churches, two doctors, a photographer and studio, silversmith, shoe store, and flourmill. The city was officially incorporated in 1882 and became the Yamhill County seat in 1886. Most of the buildings in the downtown historic district, on and around 3rd Street, were constructed between 1885 and 1912. The "gut", as locals fondly call it, still retains its turn-of-the-century charm. Annual cultural events include Turkey Rama, a festival begun more than fifty years ago that observes the county's turkey production history. The turkey farms are gone, but the "Worlds Largest Turkey Barbeque," "Turkey Trot," and street fair live on. The International Pinot Noir Celebration is held every July on the Linfield College campus. The city claims the title of "Capital of Oregon's Wine Industry" with fourteen wineries and 523 acres of grapes in the McMinnville A.V.A.

Evergreen Aviation and Space Museum

Points of Interest

• **McMinnville City Park**
(at the west end of the downtown core between 2nd and 5th on Park Drive)
The original 1910 park included a bandstand and small zoo. The city library and aquatic center are located at the eastern edge of the upper park. A millstone remnant of the Star Mill and indentations in the hillside where zoo cages once existed can be seen in the lower park.

• **McMinnville Chamber of Commerce** *(417 Adams)*
Located in a century-old house.

McMinnville

Points of Interest (continued)

- **McMinnville City Hall** (230 2nd)
  Constructed in 1928.

- **Cozine House** (105 3rd)
  1892, now the McMinnville Downtown Association Building. Nearby Cozine Creek is named for Samuel Cozine, an early pioneer in the area. The Cozines, with Mrs. P.W. Chandler, donated twenty acres of land for the Baptist College (Linfield) campus.

- **Montgomery Ward Building** (203 3rd)
  Opened in 1923.

- **Masonic Lodge** (235 3rd)
  The Mason's held their first meeting in this new lodge in 1923.

- **Schilling Building** (238 3rd)
  Possibly the oldest building in the downtown area, built around 1884 as a saloon.

- **McMinnville Bank** (250 3rd)
  Opened in 1885. Upstairs was the McMinnville Business College and a doctors office.

- **Hodson Building** (300 3rd)
  Constructed in 1902 as a hardware store. It has since been a grocery store, Sears Catalog store, a cake decorating shop and an art gallery.

- **Mardis Building** (303 3rd)
  Home to the Smith and DeHaven Hardware Store in 1912.

- **Oregon Hotel** (319 3rd)
  The two-story hotel opened in 1905. The third and fourth floors were added in 1912, making it the largest hotel in Yamhill County.

- **Campbell Building** (321 3rd)
  Originally the McMinnville Dancing Club, which opened in 1892.

- **Union Block Building** (403 3rd)
  The Kay and Todd Clothier and Tailor Shop opened in 1890.

- **Wright Building** (406 3rd)
  Built in the Queen Anne style in 1893. The name E. Wright is inscribed on the central pediment.

- **J.C. Penney Building** (448 3rd)
  Penney's opened about 1928.

- **Cook's Hotel** (502 3rd)
  This three-story hotel was built in 1886 with twenty-eight guest rooms that included a bridal suite.

- **Original Elk's Lodge Building** (516 3rd)
  1908.

- **IOOF Building** (585 3rd)
  This building opened June 26, 1909. The upstairs is now five apartments.

- **Jameson Hardware Building** (608 3rd)
  This store opened for business in 1912. The original painted sign is still visible on the east side of the building.

- **O'Dell Building** (610 3rd)
  Constructed in 1904.

- **News-Register Newspaper** (611 3rd)
  Housed here since 1908.

- **Hendershott House** (729 3rd)
  Today a restaurant, originally the finest single-family home on Third Street.

Post Office

Cozine House

- **McMinnville Train Depot**
  (741 3rd)
  The first train came to
  McMinnville in 1879. This
  building was constructed in 1912
  when the electric interurban
  service opened between Portland
  and Eugene.

- **Oregon Mutual Insurance**
  (347 4th)
  This building was constructed
  in 1922.

- **Pepsi Bottling Company**
  (980 4th)
  Began making soda in 1921.

- **Yamhill County Courthouse**
  (535 NE 5th)
  In an 1887 election, voters elected
  to relocate the county seat from
  Lafayette to McMinnville. The
  original 1889 building served until
  the current structure was built in
  1964.

- **Post Office** *(414 Evans)*
  This office opened in 1935.

- **Community Center**
  (600 NE Evans)
  Formerly an armory.

- **McMinnville Water and Light**
  (455 Irvine)
  1928.

- **Old Houses** *(Historic downtown
  area including Adams, Baker, Cowls,
  Davis, Evans and Ford streets)*
  Several have been converted into
  Bed and Breakfasts. Walking tour
  maps are available at the Cozine
  house.

- **Kiwanis Marine Park**
  (1400 NE Brooks)
  Riverside walking trails and picnic
  tables.

- **Linfield College** *(900 SE Baker)*
  One of the oldest colleges in
  the Pacific Northwest, this
  private, four-year, liberal arts and
  sciences college was chartered
  in 1858 as the Baptist College at
  McMinnville. The original school
  is rooted in the history of the
  founding of the town. The name
  was changed to Linfield College
  in 1922 after Frances Linfield
  donated property in her husband's
  memory. Pioneer Hall, the oldest
  building on campus, was built
  in 1882 and is on the National
  Register of Historic Places. It
  once housed the entire college.

- **Joe Dancer Park**
  (NE Village Court)
  A 100-acre park, named after
  a longtime city manager, that
  features soccer, baseball and
  softball fields, a playground and
  the Drew Ottley Memorial Skate
  Park.

- **Wortman Park:** *(2099 N Koch)*
  A stream runs through this large,
  forested park that features a disc
  golf course.

- **Rotary Club Nature Preserve**
  (27th and Westside Road)
  Nature paths wind through
  woods.

- **Yamhill County Fairgrounds**
  (2070 NE Lafayette Avenue)
  The Yamhill County fair is the
  oldest County Fair in Oregon
  since 1854. The fair is also host to
  an NPRA rodeo.

- **Joseph Mattey House**
  (10221 Mattey Lane)
  1892 Queen Ann Victorian on
  the National Historic Register.
  Mattey, an orphan from England
  and a butcher by trade, was a
  successful local businessman. The
  house has had several owners and
  was at one time a large strawberry
  farm. It has been a B&B since the
  mid 1980s.

- **Evergreen Aviation and Space
  Museum** *(500 NE Captain Michael
  King Smith Way)*
  Home of Howard Hughes'
  famed "Spruce Goose", an SR-71
  "Blackbird", a Titan II SLV
  Missile, and other historic and
  educational air and space artifacts
  and exhibits. The Museum
  grounds include an IMAX theater,
  Wings and Waves Waterpark,
  café's and a playground. Open
  daily 9-5.

McMinnville to Bellevue

Distance:
9.1 miles

Directions:
From the intersection of Linfield Avenue and South Baker Street, proceed south on South Baker Street (Hwy 18).

Points En Route

(mileage from intersection of Linfield Avenue and South Baker Street)

0.4 miles:
Intersection (South Baker and Old Sheridan Road) with traffic light. Turn right on Old Sheridan Road.

0.8 miles:
Turn left and stay on Old Sheridan Road.

1.0 miles:
McMinnville Grange #31, located at 1700 Old Sheridan Highway.

1.5 miles:
Turn-of-the-century farm.

2.7 miles:
Masonville Road. Turn right.

4.4 miles:
Turn left on McCabe Chapel Road as it intersects with Masonville Road. Near this intersection lies South Yamhill Cemetery, dating to the 1880s. Continue on McCabe.

4.8 miles:
McCabe Methodist Church. Constructed in 1886, this hilltop church affords a wondrous view of the valley. Note the 'His and Her' two-hole outhouse.

5.8 miles:
Intersection with Oldsville Road.

6.3 miles:
Yamhill Valley Vineyards.

7.0 miles:
Christensen Century Farm, 1902.

7.1 miles:
Erratic Rock Park. A small parking area is designated on the highway. A half-mile path leads to the many-ton giants deposited high on the hill tens of thousands of years ago. There is a picnic area that is surrounded by vineyards and affords a spectacular view of the valley.

7.4 miles:
Russell-Harding Century Farm. 1899.

7.9 miles:
Intersection of Oldsville Road and Highway 18. Turn right on Highway 18.

8.5 miles:
Bernards Farm. Originally the Duerst Farm constructed more than 100 years ago.

9.1 miles:
Bellevue

McCabe Methodist Church

Erratic Rock Park

Bellevue

Elevation: 192 feet

Location:
45.06.559 N • 123.18.542 W

Services:
food

Bellevue was named for the grand view it afforded early settlers. Hathaway Yocum, who came from Illinois, settled here in 1851. The post office opened under the name of 'Muddy' in 1869 and closed in 1904. The old schoolhouse, which is painted fire-engine-red and stands approximately a quarter-mile south of the old town site, is the last building alerting the traveler to the community's location.

Bellevue School

Points of Interest

- **Lawrence Gallery**
  (19700 Highway 18)
  Contains a variety of work by numerous renowned artists. Small picnic area.

- **Fire's Eye Gallery**
  (19915 Muddy Valley Road)
  Pottery.

- **United Brethren Cemetery**
  (north and west on SW Muddy Valley Road)
  A pioneer cemetery that dates to the 1880s.

Bellevue to Sheridan

Distance:
3.5 miles

Directions:
From the intersection of SW Muddy Valley Road and Highway 18, travel south and west toward Sheridan.

Points En Route

(mileage from the intersection of SW Muddy Valley and Highway 18 at the Lawrence Gallery)

0.3 miles:
Old Bellevue School. The sign on the building dates the construction to 1909.

0.6 miles:
Stastney Gallery.

2.7 miles:
Turn right onto the Sheridan-Willamina Business Loop Road. (Exit 34)

3.5 miles:
Sheridan

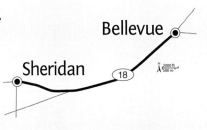

Sheridan

Elevation: 189 feet

Location:
45.05.544 N • 123.23.501 W

Services:
gas, food, lodging, B&B

Located on the South Yamhill River, Sheridan was named for Lt. Philip Henry Sheridan, a union commander during the Civil War who, from 1855-1857, served at Fort Vancouver as well as nearby Fort Grande Ronde and Fort Hoskins. Thomas Faulconer, for whom the town's elementary school is named, settled here in 1847 and founded the town in 1866, the same year the post office opened. The first merchandise store opened in 1850, owned and operated by Abe and Mose Weil. The first church, the Christian Church, was built along the river in the same year. A narrow gauge railroad connected Sheridan and Willamina in 1879. The city incorporated in 1880, was devastated by fires in 1913, 1922, and 1934, and survived serious flooding in 1964. The Federal Correctional Facility, which opened in 1989, is the city's largest employer. Sheridan was once known for its production of plums and hops. Each June, the community celebrates Phil Sheridan Days.

Heider Building

Points of Interest

- **City Hall** *(120 SW Mill)*
  Exquisitely refurbished, this former train depot, complete with ticket counter and window, was moved to this location.

- **Blackwell House**
  (144 SE Sheridan)
  This craftsman was constructed in 1915.

- **Payne House** *(244 SE Sheridan)*
  Dates to about 1910.

- **Ladd House** *(228 SE Jefferson)*
  Dates to 1910.

- **Bushman House**
  (246 SW Jefferson)
  Built in 1910 by George Bushman, who owned and operated Yamhill Milling.

- **Sleppy House** *(236 SW Water)*
  This Victorian was built in 1887. Sleppy owned the local sawmill.

- **Valley Maid Dairy and Creamery** *(Bridge)*
  Now home to Hearth and Heating.

- **Sheridan State Bank**
  (148 S Bridge)
  Opened in 1928.

- **Heider Building**
  (215-245 S Bridge)
  Circa 1925. This is the largest commercial building in Sheridan and housed the hardware store, feed store, and auto parts store. The IOOF met upstairs.

- **Hass Building** *(226 S Bridge)*
  Constructed in 1914. The owners of the drugstore lived above their business.

- **UMC Parsonage** *(244 N Bridge)*
  Built in 1920.

- **Foster House** *(246 NE Faulconer)*
  1885 construction. It is the only remaining Gothic Revival home in Sheridan.

- **Harty House** *(309 SW Madison)*
  Build for millwright William Harty in 1910.

- **Mennonite Church**
  (346 Madison)
  Constructed in 1920.

- **Old Church** (*220 SW Monroe*)
  Now a private residence.

- **Graves House** (*231 SW Monroe*)
  A craftsman home built in 1917.

- **Old Sheridan Hotel**
  (*147 NE Yamhill*)
  Built in 1892, it also served as a
  boarding house. Today a private
  residence.

- **Huntley Building**
  (*110-130 E Main*)
  Built in 1935 after fire destroyed
  the previous building.

- **Otto Heider House**
  (*440 E Main*)
  1925.

- **Hansen House** (*742 E Main*)
  Built in 1935 for Doris Hansen,
  daughter of the Chevrolet
  Dealer. Unusual Spanish Eclectic
  contruction.

- **Delphian School**
  (*20950 SW Rock Creek Road*)
  Formerly the 1930 St. Francis
  Xavier's Novitiate, now a private
  school for Scientologists.

Sheridan to Willamina

Distance:
4.0 miles

Directions:
From the light at W Main
(Highway 18) and Bridge Street,
travel west toward Willamina.

Points En Route

*(mileage from the stop light at Main
and Bridge)*

1.2 miles:
Former Otto Heider Estate,
now a B&B.

1.5 miles:
Operational lumber mill.

1.7 miles:
Farmhouse with water tower on
Mill Creek.

3.3 miles:
Former Boise Cascade Mill.

3.9 miles:
Former Georgia Pacific
Plywood Mill.

4.0 miles:
Willamina

Sleppy House

farmhouse near Sheridan

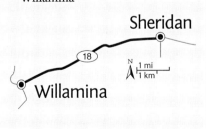

Willamina

Elevation: 225 feet

Location:
45.06.363 N • 123.29.602 W

Services:
gas, food, lodging

The name Willamina – for Willamina Williams Maley – was first given to the creek that passes through the town. Legend says that Willamina was the first white woman to ride a horse across the creek. In 1846 she came to Oregon with her husband, who died in 1847, leaving Willamina and a daughter. The Willamina Creek Post office opened in 1855. The first sawmill and gristmill started in 1878 and the town incorporated in 1903. A major brick plant operated from 1907-1974 and is said to have made many of the cream colored bricks used to construct buildings in downtown Portland. The timber industry caught hold in the 1930s, with several mills running twenty-four hours a day for many years. Six small city parks include one with a stocked fishing pond.

Willamina Museum

Points of Interest

- **Willamina Bank Building**
  (*Main and B*)
  The old 1910 bank is undergoing major renovation.

- **Willamina Movie Theatre**
  (*131 Main*)
  Opened in the 1920's and is now a hardware store.

- **Wildwood Hotel** (*150 Main*)
  Turn of the 20th Century construction, the hotel was recently remodeled.

- **Willamina Marketplace**
  (*180 Main*)
  Formerly the Willamina Post Office.

- **Dr. Andrew Kershaw House**
  (*472 Main*)
  1907. Kershaw served the Grand Ronde Reservation as physician and superintendent in the late 1800s. He is identified with various Willamina enterprises including a general mercantile store, a brick company, and the Sheridan-Willamina Railroad Company.

Dr. Andrew Kershaw House

- **IOOF Hall** (*282 Main*)
  The Odd Fellow's began meeting here in the 1890s. Today, it is a pizza parlor.

- **Old Blacksmith Shop** (*352 B*)
  The small brick structure was built to withstand a potential fire.

- **City Hall** (*411 C*)
  Constructed of locally manufactured brick.

- **Willamina Museum** (*188 D*)
  Housed in the 1887 Congregation Church building, the museum is open weekends.

- **Free Methodist Church** (*253 D*)
  Constructed in 1937.

- **Willamina Cemetery**
  (*south of the river on Pioneer Drive and Cherry*)
  Dates to the 1870s.

- **Oaken Hills Memorial Park**
  (*3rd*)
  Small park in the midst of trees.

- **Old Willamina High School Gym** (*172 NW 4th*)
  Dates to the 1920s. Fire destroyed the school in the 1980s.

- **Lamson Park** (*Lamson Street*)
  Picnic area.

- **Huddleston Pond Park**
  (*site of the old mill pond*)
  Stocked fishing pond, picnic tables and wildlife.

- **Garden Spot Park**
  (*Main and Highway 18*)
  A small park on Willamina Creek.

IOOF Hall

Log Truck in Willamina

Willamina to Blaine

Distance:
24.5 miles

Directions:
From Main and Highway 18 at Garden Spot Park, travel west on Main, which will become SW Willamina Creek Road.

Points En Route

(mileage from the intersection of Main and Highway 18)

0.3 miles:
Willamina Lumber Company.

2.2 miles:
The 1903 Fendall Creek School, District #73.

4.5 miles:
Blackwell Park. Restrooms, picnicking and fishing.

5.2 miles:
Upper Willamina Cemetery. (Buck Hollow Cemetery). Take the right turn and go up the hill to visit this cemetery.

6.1 miles:
Intersection of Willamina Creek Road and Coast Creek Road. Turn left on Coast Creek Road.

7.3 miles:
Turn right on Gilbert Creek Road.

10.5 miles:
OHV Area.

11.4 miles:
Turn left on Bible Creek Road.

12.6 miles:
Niagra Falls Access Road to the left. Stay on Bible Creek Road.

14.7 miles:
Small waterfall with pullout.

16.3 miles:
Stop sign. Turn left on the Upper Nestucca River Access Road. Information kiosk.

17.9 miles:
Rocky Creek Campground. Primitive facilities.

22.9 miles:
Blaine Fire Hall. The hall also serves as a trailhead and river access location.

24.5 miles:
Blaine

Blaine

N
2 mi
2 km

Willamina

road near Blaine

Blaine

Elevation: 480 feet

Location:
45.27.2541 N • 123.70.333 W

Services:
none

Blaine was named by the first post-master, William Smith, to honor James G. Blaine (1830-1893), a one-time Republican candidate for the presidency of the United States. To the immediate north of Blaine is Trask Mountain and to the south, Bald Peak. Blaine is located on the Nestucca River, named for the Nestucca tribe of Native Americans who lived on its banks.

Former Blaine Store

Points of Interest

- **Former Blaine Store**
  (32135 Upper Nestucca Road)
  The store is now a private residence.

Blaine to Beaver

Distance:
6.4 miles

Directions:
From intersection of Upper Nestucca Road and Moon Creek, travel west on Blaine Road. (Upper Nestucca Road)

Points En Route

(mileage from the former Blaine Store)

This route follows the Nestucca River, noted for its excellent salmon and steelhead runs.

0.3 miles:
Blaine Community Church, 31650 Upper Nestucca River Road.

6.4 miles:
Beaver

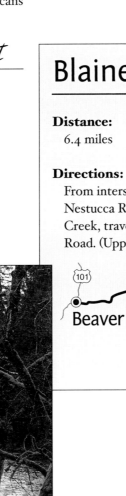

Nestucca River

Beaver

Elevation: 89 feet

Location:
45.16.363 N • 123.49.350 W

Services:
food

Crossing this section of the Coast Range from west to east takes you to the community of Beaver, which lies at the junction of Blaine Road and Highway 101. Beaver is one of the many Oregon place names influenced by the great number of beavers – *Castor canadensis* – that once thrived in this area and throughout the state. The Beaver post office opened in 1889.

Points of Interest

- **Old Beaver School**
  (near the intersection of Highway 101 and Blaine Road)
  Dates to 1913.

- **Beaver Post Office**
  (24375 Highway 101)
  Part of a multi-store complex.

- **Beaver Creek Mercantile**
  (24747 Highway 101)
  This former cheese factory and mercantile store is currently under restoration.

Beaver Creek Mercantile

Beaver Post Office

Beaver to Hebo

Distance:
4.2 miles

Directions:
From the intersection of Highway 101 and Blaine Road, travel south on Highway 101.

Points En Route

(mileage from Fox Grocery Store)

1.2 miles:
101 Camp.

2.3 miles:
Panther Creek Wayside with boat trailer parking.

4.2 miles:
Hebo

Hebo

Elevation: 77 feet

Location:
45.13.491 N • 123.51.479 W

Services:
gas, food, lodging

Hebo was named after the nearby 3153 foot Hebo Mountain by pioneer Warren Vaughn. Hebo never incorporated but has had a post office since 1882. The Hebo School opened in 1906.

Hebo Inn

Points of Interest

- **Former Hebo Gas Station**
  (31020 Highway 101)
  Now a bait and tackle shop.

- **Hebo Inn** *(31035 Highway 101)*
  The 1933 building is under renovation.

- **Hebo School #135** *(intersection of Highway 22 and Highway 101)*
  The 1906 school is now a private residence. A 1920s gym stands behind the old schoolhouse.

- **Hebo Ranger Station**
  (31525 Highway 22)
  Permits, maps, and information. The road to Hebo Lake is near this station.

- **Hebo Lake** *(4.4 miles en route to the Observatory)*
  Year 'round fishing.

- **Hebo Observatory**
  (13.2 miles on Highway 22)
  This installation gives weather and has military tracking capability. With an elevation of 3,154 feet, the top of this mountain affords a stunning view of mountains and sea. The road is not maintained during the winter months.

Hebo Lake

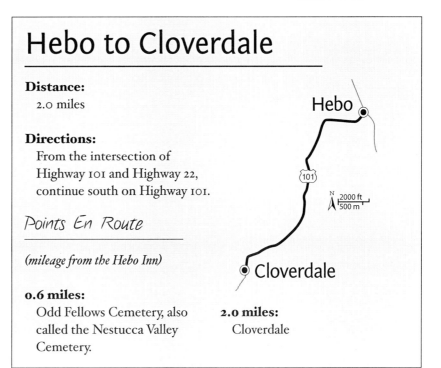

Hebo to Cloverdale

Distance:
  2.0 miles

Directions:
  From the intersection of Highway 101 and Highway 22, continue south on Highway 101.

Points En Route

(mileage from the Hebo Inn)

0.6 miles:
  Odd Fellows Cemetery, also called the Nestucca Valley Cemetery.

2.0 miles:
  Cloverdale

Cloverdale

Elevation: 26 feet

Location:
45.12.212 N • 123.53.317 W

Services:
food

Charles Ray settled in this area in 1884, working a farm that later became the site of the community. Ray established a store, hotel, bank, and a cheese factory here. Cloverdale is named after a community of the same name in California. The post office opened in 1899. At one time, Cloverdale had a hotel, confectionery, mercantile store, hardware store, cheese factory and butcher shop. Many of the shops existed, side by side, along busy Highway 101. Lush pasture land and heavy rainfall make dairy farming a major industry in the area.

Cloverdale

Points of Interest

- **Cloverdale Baptist Church**
  (34465 Bridge)
  This venerable old building was constructed in 1897.

- **St. Joseph's Catholic Church**
  (Parkway and Bridge)
  Built in 1921, it commands a nice view of the river and the town below.

- **Charles Ray House**
  (34335 Highway 101)
  The 1900 home of the town founder.

- **Old Barber Shop**
  (34360 Highway 101)
  Empty.

- **Cloverdale Visitors Center**
  (34370 Highway 101)
  The visitor's center is located in one of the old downtown businesses. The building next to the visitor's center was the William High Drug Store. Photos of the old store can be seen in the 1920 pharmacy located across the street.

- **Old downtown store**
  (34380 Highway 101)
  Note the false front addition.

- **Abandoned Church**
  (34505 Highway 101)
  A magnificent structure in its day.

Cloverdale to Pacific City

Distance:
4.9 miles

Directions:
From the intersection of Highway 101 and Bridge Street, proceed south on Highway 101 toward Pacific City.

Points En Route

(mileage from the bridge)

1.4 miles:
Nestucca Valley Elementary School.

2.3 miles:
Hudson House Bed and Breakfast. John Hudson came to the area in 1887, moving from Dayton, Oregon. He served in the Civil War and is buried, along with his family members, in the cemetery located above his home.

2.7 miles:
Turn right on Brooten Road.

3.2 miles:
Eagle's View Bed and Breakfast.

4.9 miles:
Pacific City

Pacific City

Elevation: 22 feet

Location:
45.12.901 N • 123.57.382 W

Services:
gas, food, lodging, camping, RV, B&B

Pacific City is named for its proximity to the Pacific Ocean. Platted under the name of Ocean Park in 1893, the name changed to Pacific City when the post office opened in 1909. The first school in Pacific City opened in 1910. The downtown borders the Nestucca River rather than the ocean. The town has gradually spread toward the sea and the Cape Kiwanda area is the present population hub. The Killamooks and Nestugga Indians were the first peoples in the area, with whites settling here in the 1870s.

Cape Kiwanda and a Pacific City beach

Points of Interest

- **Nestucca Bay** (*Brooten Road follows the river on the way to town*) This estuary and its wetlands are home to many species of birds and wildlife. Many people try their luck at salmon and steelhead fishing in these waters.

- **Cape Kiwanda**
Cape Kiwanda was originally known as Sand Cape, named for the nearby sand dunes that are among the most climbed on the Oregon Coast. The cape received its name from the chief of the local Nestucca Indians, Kiwanda. The dory fleet – a dory is a lightweight fishing boat, approximately 15-22 feet in length, characterized by a flat bottom whose fore and aft are angled at about 30 degrees – launches from the base of the sand and cape. Whales are frequently spotted less than one-quarter mile offshore in front of Haystack Rock. Hang gliders launch from the dunes, and wind surfers frequent the calmer, somewhat protected waters nearby. The area is one of the most photographed on the Oregon Coast.

- **Cape Kiwanda Natural Area** (*north end of Pacific City on McPhillips Drive*)
Hike, climb, picnic, swim, windsurf. The park area extends more than six miles from the cape, almost touching the community of Sandlake to the north.

- **Haystack Rock**
This famous monolith stands 327 feet tall, almost 100 feet higher than its other coastal namesake. Three geologic features share this name; the second near Cannon Beach and the third in Wallowa County. This Haystack Rock, home to numerous seabirds, was formed of basalt and has resisted millennia of erosion.

- **Dory Launching**
Anglers launch their dories into the surf to fish the rich offshore grounds.

- **Whale Watching**
Whales frequent the areas around Cape Kiwanda and Haystack Rock.

- **Hudson House Bed and Breakfast.**
(*1.5 miles south on Highway 101*)
John Hudson came to the area in 1887, moving from Dayton, Oregon. He served in the Civil War and is buried, along with his family members, in the cemetery located above his home.

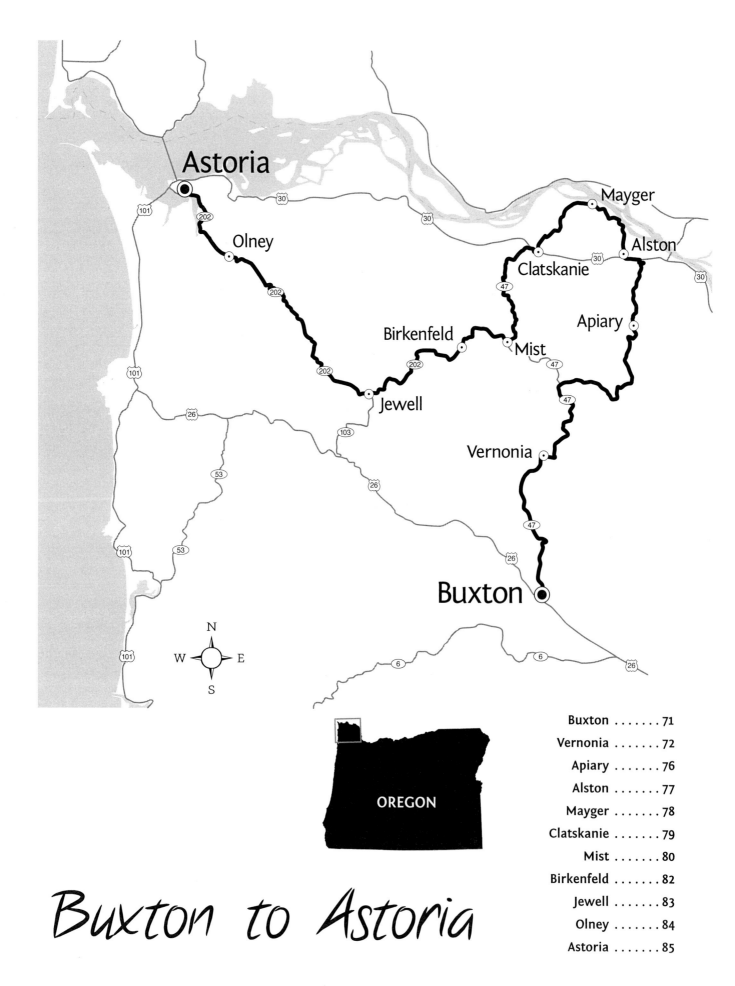

Astoria

Mayger

Alston

Clatskanie

Apiary

Birkenfeld

Mist

Olney

Jewell

Vernonia

Buxton

N
W E
S

OREGON

Buxton 71

Vernonia 72

Apiary 76

Alston 77

Mayger 78

Clatskanie 79

Mist 80

Birkenfeld 82

Jewell 83

Olney 84

Astoria 85

Buxton to Astoria

69

It's a Long Way to Apiary

Buxton to Astoria (111 miles)

Breathtaking views of rivers, mountains, and ocean can be found on back roads between Buxton and Astoria, an area of small towns born from Oregon's pioneer spirit. This excursion crosses the Coast Range (twice), follows the mighty Columbia River, and ends near the Pacific Ocean, affording much evidence of Oregon's former major economies of lumbering and fishing.

In addition, several alternative roads and side trips line this route, offering further opportunities for exploration of communities that once thrived before the decline of the timber industry. Slow down, explore, and listen for echoes of the past in places seemingly bypassed by progress and time. Begin this adventure twenty-miles west of Portland in the community of Buxton, located on Highway 47 via Fischer Road off the Sunset Highway (US Highway 26).

bridge over Columbia River at Astoria

Buxton

Elevation: 332 feet

Location:
45.41.233 N • 123.11.234 W

Services:
gas, food

Adventurous people with great aspirations for a better tomorrow first settled here. One of these was the town's namesake, Henry Buxton, who arrived in 1842, and whose son Henry T. became the community's first postmaster in 1886. The post office closed abruptly in 1976 and the town never incorporated. Even though the noisy mills and log-truck caravans that once funneled economic life into this logging community are now gone, and even though some of its streets and homes need repair, the community still dreams of a brighter future. As many as seven sawmills operated in the area during the heyday of the timber industry.

Buxton Food and Feed

Points of Interest

- **Buxton School**
  (22785 NW Fischer)
  Dates to 1922. Now the private Banks Christian Academy.

- **Buxton Food and Feed**
  (22915 NW Fischer)
  Once the mercantile, now a crafts store.

- **Assembly of God Church**
  (23025 NW Fischer)
  Early 20th century construction.

- **Banks to Vernonia Linear Trail** *(begins at the Assembly of God Church)*
  Travel by foot, bike, or horse from Banks to Vernonia along a former rail line with retrofitted trestles. The trail, which is well maintained and handicapped accessible, frequently crosses the highway.

- **Buxton Community Cemetery** *(cross Highway 26 to Strassel Road - near the junction of Highway 26 and Highway 47)*
  Dates to 1890.

Assembly of God Church

Buxton to Vernonia

Distance:
13.7 miles

Directions:
From the Buxton Feed Store, drive North on NW Fisher Road, heading toward the Assembly of God Church.

Points En Route

(mileage from the Buxton Feed Store)

0.05 miles:
Turn left on NW Fisher (Assembly of God Church).

0.3 miles:
Railroad Tracks. Turn right on Highway 47, the Nehalem Highway.

3.9 miles:
L.L. "Stub" Stewart State Park. Year-round camping on over 1,600 acres of lush rolling hills, forests, and deep canyons.

5.8 miles:
Banks-Vernonia Linear Park Trailhead. Top Hill Trailhead.

7.6 miles:
Enter Columbia County.

8.6 miles:
Former Treharne School, now a private residence.

9.9 miles:
Banks-Vernonia Linear Park access. Beaver Creek Trailhead.

12.9 miles:
Crossing the Nehalem River.

13.7 miles:
Vernonia

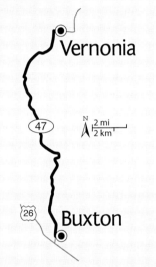

Vernonia

Elevation: 660 feet

Location:
45.51.355 N • 123.11.288 W

Services:
gas, food, lodging, B&B, RV

In 1874, the Clark Parker and Van Blaricom families first settled here with Ohio cousins Judson Weed and Ozias Cherrington following in 1876. In need of a post office, Cherrington suggested the name of Vernona, after his daughter who was living in Ohio. Postal authorities accepted the name in 1878, but misspelled it, instead naming it Vernonia. Ozias, whose daughter never came to Oregon, died of an accident in 1894, not seeing her again. The community officially incorporated in 1891. Vernonia was a timber town that grew rapidly when the railroad came through in 1924 and the state-of-the-art Oregon American Mill opened. The town thrived, supporting three car dealerships, a Safeway, and a JC Penney department store, as well as several hotels. The last old growth timber was harvested and the old mill closed in 1957. At one time, the mill was the world's largest electrically operated sawmill. Unfortunately, Vernonia has been hit with major floods, one in 1996 and another in 2007. Major flood damage made it necessary to rebuild and relocate the school that opened in 2009. The small community has six parks, some of which provide RV hook-ups. Old steam locomotive #102 rests in Shay Park.

Points of Interest

- **City Hall** *(1001 Bridge)*
  New construction.

- **Doc Eby's office** *(953 Bridge)*
  1922. Also served as a dentist office and an insurance office and now a realty office.

Vernonia City Hall

Vernonia

Points of Interest (continued)

- **Former Safeway Store** (*919 Bridge*)
  First a Piggly Wiggly in 1924, then Safeway in 1935. Today, a restaurant and brewery.

- **Bank of Vernonia** (*905 Bridge*)
  Opened in 1926.

- **JC Penny Building**
  (*884/886 Bridge*)
  1930.

- **Nehalem Market** (*825 Bridge*)
  Opened in 1920.

- **Bush Furniture** (*805 Bridge*)
  1923.

- **Stuart Block** (*791 Bridge*)
  One of the first buildings to be constructed of brick after fires took their toll on wood structures. 1920.

- **Vernonia Power and Light**
  (*622 Bridge*)
  Built in 1924.

- **Oregon American Mill Office**
  (*511 Bridge*)
  1924.

- **Emil Malmsten House** (*291 A*)
  Built by early settler Malmsten in 1918.

Grandma Lamping House

1st Baptist Church

- **Bergerson Building** (*879 Bridge*)
  Originally a hardware store.

- **Palace Café** (*859 Bridge*)
  Opened as a café and also housed the bus station, a TV repair shop, and an appliance store.

- **Vernonia Variety** (*847 Bridge*)
  Best known as Steers Variety, opening in 1920.

- **Brickel Building** (*831 Bridge*)
  This building, constructed in 1910, has been a barbershop, dress shop and a variety store.

- **The Card Room** (*748 Bridge*)
  This 1923 business is now the Cedar Side Inn.

- **Brunsman Hardware**
  (*736 Bridge*)
  1915.

- **Mike's Tavern** (*733 Bridge*)
  Opened in 1910.

- **Nance's Drug Store** (*725 Bridge*)
  The local newspaper is printed in this 1910 building.

- **Joy Theater** (*711 Bridge*)
  This 1926 theater played its first "talkie" in 1929.

- **Palace Café** (*859 B*)
  Opened in 1920.

- **Grandma Lamping House**
  (*758 Weed*)
  One of the oldest homes in Vernonia, built in 1879.

- **IOOF Building** (*500 North*)
  Constructed in 1920 and now serves as a church.

- **Vernonia Grange** (*375 North*)
  Built in 1907 and moved twice.

- **Grandma Rogers House** (*362 North*)
  Built in 1906 as her home and birthing center.

- **Vernonia Inn** (*900 Madison*)
  The 1925 Hy Van Hotel was remodeled and converted into a Bed and Breakfast.

- **Vernonia Mortuary** (*741 Madison*)
  In business since 1925.

- **Vernonia Eagle** (*725 Madison*)
  Built in 1925 and now Leonetti's Restaurant.

- **Crawford Motors** (*735 Jefferson*)
  Originally the Ford Dealership in 1930.

- **Old Arkansas Inn** (*487 Mill*)
  Another building converted into a Bed and Breakfast.

- **Sturdevant Building** (*717 Rose*)
  Originally the Vernonia Brazing Works (machine shop).

- **Rock Creek B&B** (*1162 State*)
  A spacious, single room, overnight accomodation.

- **Andersen House** (*1206 State*)
  Built in 1906.

- **Evangelical Church** (*957 State*)
  Opened in 1924; now the Vernonia Community Church.

- **Scout Cabin** (*901 Park*)
  Originally constructed for Camp Fire Girls in 1920.

- **Vernonia Pioneer Museum** (*511 E Bridge*)
  Free admission and open weekends. The building was part of the Oregon-American Mill.

- **Vernonia Pioneer Cemetery** (*follow State to Keasey*)
  Dates to the 1890s.

- **Hall-Tipton Cemetery** (*Alder and Polk*)
  1919.

- **Vernonia Memorial Cemetery** (*2080 Bridge*)
  Located on Corey Hill, this cemetery dates to 1910.

Vernonia Pioneer Museum

Craftsman house in Vernonia

Vernonia to Apiary

Distance:
21.9 miles

Directions:
From the bridge over Rock Creek at Shay Park, drive north on Bridge Street (Highway 47 - the Nehalem Highway) toward Apiary.

Points En Route

(mileage from the bridge over Rock Creek)

0.5 miles:
Vernonia Pioneer Museum.

0.8 miles:
Vernonia Lake Park (site of the American Mill).

0.9 miles:
Crossing the Nehalem River. Note the construction of homes, built to handle frequent flooding.

1.7 miles:
Red barn with cupola.

2.6 miles:
Crossing the Nehalem River.

2.9 miles:
Road to Keasey, a former logging community located a dozen miles up Keasey Road. Keasey was named for an early settler.

4.4 miles:
Crossing the Nehalem River.

4.5 miles:
Site of Pittsburg. Pittsburg was named after the steel-producing city in Pennsylvania. Peter Brous, who hailed from the Keystone State, built a water-powered gristmill and sawmill at this site. In 1879, he was named the postmaster of Pittsburgh. The name was changed to Pittsburg in 1892, though the reason for dropping the "h" is unknown. The post office ceased to operate in 1908, and today a few homes and a restaurant are all that remain of this once lively logging camp. Locals say the food at the restaurant is excellent and abundant, a throwback to its logging past. The 1996 and 2007 floods did much damage to many homes located near the river.

5.0 miles:
Veer left on Highway 47 toward Mist and Clatskanie.

7.8 miles:
Big Eddy County Park. Located on the Nehalem River, this park features a museum and old growth trees.

8.7 miles:
Wilkerson turn-off Road. Turn right toward Apiary and Rainier.

12.3 miles:
Rock quarry.

14.4 miles:
Camp Wilkerson Park and the site of Wilkerson, a short-lived logging community.

16.3 miles:
Nichols Tree Farm.

20.6 miles:
Stay left on Apiary Road.

21.5 miles:
Intersection with Fern Hill Road. Travel 0.6 miles to the 1898 Apiary Cemetery.

21.9 miles:
Apiary

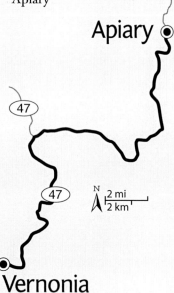

Nehalem River

Apiary

Elevation: 984 feet

Location:
46.01.811 N • 123.01.549 W

Services:
none

Apiary is the only community in the United States named for bee ranching. It is said that postmaster David Dorsey had many beehives that produced much honey, prompting the name for the community. There has been continuous honey farming at Apiary since 1889, and one current resident has bee-ranched for more than fifty years. As did many communities in these mountains, Apiary lived and died with the timber industry, and today only a few scattered homes remain. The post office opened in 1889 and closed in 1924. A steam driven sawmill was located here in 1911.

Points of Interest

- **Apiary School** (*near intersection of Apiary Road and Fern Hill Road*) The 1918 school has been converted to a private residence.

Apiary School

Apiary to Alston

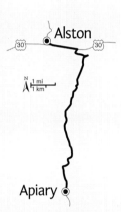

Distance:
9.3 miles

Directions:
From the intersection of Apiary Road and Simmons Road (at the former schoolhouse), continue north on Apiary Road.

Points En Route

(*mileage from the former Apiary School*)

3.2 miles:
Geodesic dome house. One of several in the area.

5.5 miles:
Intersection with the old Rainier Highway. Turn right and proceed toward Alston.

6.3 miles:
Hudson Parcher County Park. Site of Hudson, which had its own post office from 1892 to 1913. At this intersection, turn left on Larson Road. The road sign may be missing.

6.6 miles:
The 1879 Woodbine Cemetery, 1906 Green Mountain Cemetery and across the street is the newer Hudson Cemetery.

6.7 miles:
Beaver Valley Grange #306.

6.9 miles:
Intersection with new Highway 30. At the stop, turn left on new Highway 30 and then take a quick right turn on Wonderly Road, Old Highway 30.

8.1 miles:
Four-way stop. Continue straight.

9.3 miles:
Alston

Alston

Elevation: 527 feet

Location:
46.09.911 N • 123.04.704 W

Services:
food

Alston sits more than five hundred feet above the Columbia River and developed around the traffic of Highway 30. Lumber, once the main economy, has given way to agriculture, especially dairy products. Several churches, a bank, restaurant, and private residences make Alston a worthwhile stop. Alston was named for a pioneer family.

Points of Interest

- **Old Store and Gas Station**
  (25240 Old Highway 30)
  Across from the new store.

Old store and gas station

Alston to Mayger

Distance:
6.5 miles

Directions:
From the intersection of the Alston-Mayger Road and Old Highway 30, proceed north on the Alston-Mayger Highway.

Points En Route

(mileage from the Alston Store)

2.5 miles:
Million-dollar view of the Columbia River.

3.1 miles:
Old farmhouse with a view of the river.

5.5 miles:
Mayger-Downing Community Church. Turn of the century construction.

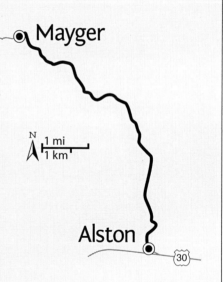

6.1 miles:
Mayger Cemetery, 1890s.

6.3 miles:
Turn right on Mayger Fill Road.

6.5 miles:
Mayger

Mayger

Elevation: 19 feet

Location:
46.16,304 N • 123.10.698 W

Services:
none

C.W. Mayger, a native of France, came to Oak Point, Washington, in about 1865, settling in what is now Mayger. The post office was established in 1889 and Mayger served as postmaster in the town named for him. The office closed seventy-two years later in 1961. The community was originally located nearer the river, and at one time millions of pounds of salmon were processed at its fish docks. Frequent flooding eventually resulted in the town moving to higher ground. Pilings from the old canneries can still be seen as they slowly deteriorate in the water.

Points of Interest

- **Fish Cannery** (*pilings visible in the river off Fish Station Road*)
  Millions of pounds of salmon were processed in this abandoned building.

Quincy School

Fish Cannery

Mayger to Clatskanie

Distance:
6.7 miles

Directions:
From the river, backtrack 0.2 miles to the Quincy-Mayger Road, Old Highway 30.

Points En Route

(*mileage from the river*)

0.2 miles:
Turn right on Quincy-Mayger Road.

0.4 miles:
Former Mayger School, now a private residence.

1.0 miles:
Kalluni Road. The location of Fanny's Bottom, site of Nathan Winship's 1810 landing. Winship was a sea captain from Boston who built a fort near this spot.

2.6 miles:
A former school, now Great Vow Zen Monastery.

3.4 miles:
Quincy General Store. The store may not be old, but many of the buildings near it are. J.W. Barnes, an early settler who hailed from Quincy, Illinois, named Quincy. The town was platted in 1882 and the post office established ten years later.

4.1 miles:
1925 Quincy School. This magnificent two-story structure now serves as a storage unit.

5.4 miles:
Apostolic Lutheran Church.

6.3 miles:
Old general store-hardware store and badminton bird burner.

6.7 miles:
Clatskanie

Clatskanie

Elevation: 15 feet

Location:
46.10.111 N • 123.12.359 W

Services:
gas, food, B&B

Tlatskanie or Tlatskanai may have been the tribal name of the Native Americans who lived in this area, though some say that *Tlastkani* is an Athapascan word that means "swift running water." White settlers used the word to describe the river rather than the process of getting here. The town was platted where the Clatskanie River joins the Columbia. Historical sources as early as 1852 say the community was called "Bryantville" for E.G. Bryant, whose land claim was the site upon which the small settlement grew. The name was changed to Clatskanie in 1870 and the town incorporated in 1891. The last native Clatskanie Indian passed away in 1910. Clatskanie has a rich lumber and logging heritage, and even though a couple of lumber mills continue to produce wood products, production is far less than in years past. Instead, the town's economy today is anchored in the pulp and paper industry. The Trojan Nuclear Power plant provided many jobs in the area until it closed in the 1980s. Many areas for bird watching exist near the river.

Flippin Castle

Points of Interest

- **Benson House** (*5th and Nehalem*)
Overlooks the downtown, built in 1903.

- **Clatskanie Bank**
(*Steele and Nehalem*)
Today the Sterling Savings Bank.

- **IOOF Building** (*65 Nehalem*)
Under major reconstruction.

- **Clatskanie Presbyterian Church** (*215 Nehalem*)
Opened in 1899.

- **Bryant House** (*265 Nehalem*)
The 1880s home of the town founder.

- **Clatskanie United Methodist Church** (*290 Nehalem*)
Built in 1894.

- **Masonic Lodge #133** (*165 2nd*)
1908.

- **Flippin Castle** (*620 SW Tichenor*)
This beautiful Victorian, built by early lumberman T.J. Flippin, serves today as the Clatskanie Senior Center.

- **Bryant Cemetery / Cedar Hill Cemetery** (*800 NE Wood Lane*)
Town founder E.G. Bryant is buried here. Bryant Cemetery, 1878. Cedar Hill Cemetery, 1905.

- **Maple Wood Cemetery**
(*858 SE Conyers Creek Road*)
Circa 1890.

- **Murray Hill Cemetery**
(*90 SW Hall Road*)
A pioneer cemetery.

IOOF Building

Clatskanie to Mist

Distance:
10.9 miles

Directions:
From the intersection of
Highway 47 and Highway 30 at
the Safeway Store, drive west
on Highway 47 (also called
Orchard Street).

Points En Route

*(mileage from the intersection of
Highway 47 and Highway 30)*

0.2 miles:
Lovely, old homes with grand
views of the river line the road
as it leads out of town.

1.4 miles:
Palm Hill Road State Forestry
guard station.

5.0 miles:
Dense forest.

7.1 miles:
Incredible mountain views as
well as logging clear-cuts.

10.7 miles:
A stately Victorian at 69355
Highway 47.

10.9 miles:
Mist

Mist

Elevation: 560 feet

Location:
45.59.482 N • 123.15.191 W

Services:
food

Called Riverside as early as 1874,
Mist took its current name in 1888
from the persistent precipitation
that permeates the area. The hustle
and bustle of this former lumbering
community is gone, replaced with
the slower agrarian economy. Natural
gas fields have replaced logging as an
industry in this sleepy berg that is
home to numerous old farmsteads,
barns, and garages.

Points of Interest

• **Mist Church and Cemetery**
The church was constructed in
1883 and the cemetery had its first
burial in 1890.

• **Mist School** *(69163 Highway 47)*
Almost 100 years old. The old bell
rests in the tower.

• **Mist School Gym**
(69165 Highway 47)
Gym and community center.

• **Site of Mist General Store**
(69290 Highway 47)
The 1874 store and post office
burned to the ground in 2001. All
that remains is a sign that says
"Gasoline."

• **Mist Natural Gas Fields**
Capping stations are evidence
of the natural gas that exists in
shallow pockets, roughly 2,200
feet below the surface.

Mist School

Birkenfeld

Location:

49.99.010 N • 123.33.762 W

Services:

food

Anton Birkenfeld, a German immigrant who settled in the Nehalem Valley in 1886, founded this town on the Nehalem River twenty-four years later. The old school house, now converted to the Community Church, is the first major structure greeting travelers to Birkenfeld, a stringtown community. Sadly, the post office closed in 2010 after operating ninety-four years.

Birkenfeld Community Church

Mist to Birkenfeld

Distance:

4.8 miles

Directions:

At the intersection of Highway 47 and Highway 202, turn left onto Highway 202 toward Birkenfeld.

Points En Route

(mileage from intersection of Highway 47 and 202)

0.1 miles:

Old farmhouse.

0.5 miles:

Another old farmhouse.

1.2 miles:

Former dairy farm.

4.1 miles:

Junction with Fishhawk Lake Road. Stay on Highway 47. Fishhawk Lake Cemetery is 1.2 miles to the right.

4.8 miles:

Birkenfeld

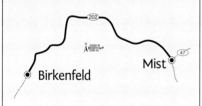

Points of Interest

- **Birkenfeld Community Church** *(11249 Highway 202)* Previously the Birkenfeld School.

- **Birkenfeld Country Store** *(11139 Highway 202)* Built in 1910, the store now sells groceries, lunch, and other necessities to residents and travelers. The second floor of the building used to be the dance hall, where many loggers and farmers could be found on a Saturday night.

- **Birkenfeld Restaurant** *(11126 Highway 202)* The restaurant was formerly the hardware store and part of the train depot. Some of the buildings around the restaurant were part of the narrow gauge railroad and roundhouse.

Birkenfeld Country Store

Birkenfeld to Jewell

Distance:
11.4 miles

Directions:
From the Birkenfeld Store, proceed south and west on Highway 202 to Jewell.

Points En Route

(mileage from the Birkenfeld Store)

0.2 miles:
Crossing the Nehalem River.

0.9 miles:
Old farmstead.

1.2 miles:
Old dairy operation.

1.7 miles:
Entering Clatsop County.

2.1 miles:
Old, picturesque church.

4.1 miles:
Sager Creek fire station.

5.7 miles:
Northup Creek. Horse Camp (4 miles on Northup Creek Rd.).

11.4 miles:
Junction of Highway 103 and Highway 202.

11.4 miles:
Jewell

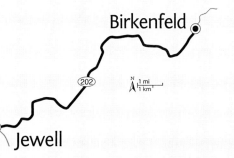

Jewell

Elevation: 480 feet

Location:
45.56.511 N • 123.30.101 W

Services:
none

Even though it was named in honor of U.S. Postmaster General Marshall Jewell in the 1870s, Jewell is a most appropriate name for this community, which is home to more elk than people. That's because nearby Jewell Meadows Wildlife Area covers more than 1,100 acres in four locations. Calves are born in mid-June. Look for black tail deer, red-tailed hawks, bald eagles, coyotes, raccoons, a variety of songbirds, and species of duck. Douglas fir, western hemlock, red alder, and maple trees surround the wetland meadows. The Jewell post office opened in 1874 and closed in 1967.

Points of Interest

- **Jewell Schools**
  (83874 Highway 103)
  The first school opened in 1874, this one in 1916.

Elk near Jewell

Abandoned Storefront

Jewell to Olney

Distance:
18.7 miles

Directions:
From the intersection of Highway 202 and Highway 103, drive west on Highway 202 toward Astoria.

Points En Route

(mileage from intersection of Highway 202 and Highway 103)

0.1 miles:
Former Jewell garage, now a rubble heap.

0.7 miles:
Clatsop County Sheriff's office.

1.0 miles:
Jewell Meadows Viewing Area I.

1.3 miles:
Jewell Meadows Viewing Area II. An old farmhouse serves as the wildlife center.

1.7 miles:
Wildlife viewing area III.

2.3 miles:
Wildlife viewing area IV.

4.0 miles:
Lee Wooden Park and Fishhawk Creek Waterfall (100 feet).

16.8 miles:
Klatskanine Fish Hatchery.

16.9 miles:
Leahy Homestead and barn. Built in 1879.

17.3 miles:
RV Park.

17.9 miles:
Olney Lane. This is a loop road that comes out at the Olney Store. It bypasses most of the community buildings and goes by an elk farm. While in the velvet-antlered stage, elk are tranquilized and their antlers removed. The antlers are then dried, ground into a powder, and sold to South East Asian markets as an aphrodisiac. The elk are not harmed and later graze alongside beef cattle behind the farm's high fences.

18.7 miles:
Olney

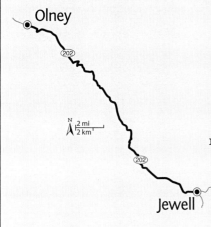

Olney

Elevation: 185 feet

Location:
46.06.011 N • 123.75.722 W

Services:
gas, food

Ohio-born Cyrus Olney was appointed the Supreme Justice of the Oregon Territory in 1853, and is honored by having this community bear his name. Olney resigned his position in 1857 to serve on Oregon's constitutional convention, and died in Astoria in 1870 at the age of fifty-five. The Olney post office operated from 1875 until 1950. The Western Cooperage Company operated in Olney from 1910 to 1943, employing as many as fifty people. Not much remains of this once thriving mill town, though the community store with its antique displays still offers respite to residents, travelers, hunters, and anglers.

Points of Interest

- **Olney Grange #793**
  (89342 Highway 202)
  Circa 1920.

- **Olney Community Church**
  (89351 Highway 202)
  This building opened in 1956.

- **Olney Store and Saloon**
  (89456 Highway 202)
  This store was constructed in 1920. The original store was destroyed by fire.

Olney Grange

Olney Store and Saloon

Olney to Astoria

Distance:
6.5 miles

Directions:
From the store, proceed north on Highway 202 toward Astoria.

Points En Route

(mileage from the Olney Store)

0.1 miles:
Old, round barn with cupola.

1.1 miles:
Stately old home with leaded glass windows.

2.4 miles:
Old farm.

2.9 miles:
Young's Bay Estuary.

3.7 miles:
Greenwood Cemetery, 1891.

4.8 miles:
Clatsop County Fairgrounds.

5.6 miles:
Grand home with a surround porch and bay view.

5.7 miles:
Pilings, like these, that once a held a salmon cannery, are present in the bay all the way to Astoria.

6.1 miles:
Clear view of the Astor Column on Coxcomb Hill.

6.5 miles:
Astoria

Pilings near Astoria

Astoria

Elevation: 19 feet

Location:
44.11.220 N • 123.49.167 W

Services:
gas, food, lodging, B&B, RV

Captain Robert Gray, the first known white man to explore the river, sailed his ship, the Columbia, to this area in 1792. Lewis and Clark explored the area in 1804-05. Astoria is the oldest U.S. settlement west of the Rocky Mountains, and was named for John Jacob Astor, investor and America's first million-aire, who established his Pacific Fur Trading Company here in 1811. Even though the outpost was renamed Fort George when the British took over during the War of 1812, the name Astoria was restored in 1818 when the U.S. reclaimed the area. The Astoria post office opened on March 9, 1847, making it not only the oldest in Oregon, but also the first on the west coast. Astoria incorporated as a city in 1876. Fires have twice destroyed the downtown, first in 1883 and again in 1922. By 1920, after rebuilding from the first fire, Astoria boasted more than 14,000 residents, but a dreadful fire in 1922 eliminated thirty-two city blocks, leaving behind little but ash and prompting more than 3,000 people to vacate the community. In 1945 more than thirty fish canneries were operating, the last closing in 1980. The last mill closed in 1989, and the Burlington Northern Railroad discontinued service in 1996. Despite this adversity, Astoria's rich history, as well as its Scandinavian culture and heritage, attracts increasing numbers of visitors. More than a dozen well-known movies have been filmed in Astoria. Clark Gable began his acting career at the Astoria Theatre in 1922.

Cargo ship near Astoria Harbor

Points of Interest

- **Astoria Maritime Memorial**
  (*200 West Marine Drive*)
  The waterfront park has three viewing areas.

- **Union Fisherman's Cannery**
  (*325 Taylor*)
  Site of the cannery that was organized and operated by Columbia River fisherman, who processed the fish they caught.

- **Columbia River Inn**
  (*495 Marine*)
  This 1870 home has been converted to an Inn.

- **Hobson House** (*469 Bond*)
  Built in 1863.

- **Job Ross House** (*817 Exchange*)
  One of Astoria's oldest residences, built of cedar in 1852.

Grace Episcopal Church

- **Flavel House** (*441 8th*)
  Built in 1885 by the Columbia River's first licensed pilot and Astoria's first millionaire, this home of elegant architecture is filled with period antiques.

- **Victorian House** (*847 8th*)
  Today, Clementine's B&B. Built in 1888. Next-door is the 1847 building that holds the Lagniappe Restaurant.

- **Shark Rock Park**
  (*8th and Niagara*)
  This rock bears a message left by the survivors of the U.S. Sloop Shark, that was wrecked at the mouth of the Columbia River on September 16, 1846.

- **Captain Eric Johnson House**
  (*960 Franklin*)
  This sea captain's home was built in 1878.

- **Dewitt Clinton Ireland House**
  (*989 Franklin*)
  Home of the newspaper publisher in 1870.

- **Methodist Church**
  (*1076 Franklin*)
  Established in 1840 by Jason Lee, this building opened in 1916.

- **First Presbyterian Church**
  (*1103 Grand*)
  This building was constructed in 1903 but the church was established in 1877.

- **Liberty Theatre**
  (*1203 Commercial*)
  The 1925 theater has been restored.

- **Hotel Elliot** (*357 12th*)
  Constructed in 1924 and renovated in 2003.

- **John Quincy Adams Bowlby House** (*1229 Franklin*)
  Built for the attorney in 1870.

- **Captain Hiram Brown House**
  (*1337 Franklin*)
  The oldest home in Astoria, built for this sea captain in 1852.

Flavel House

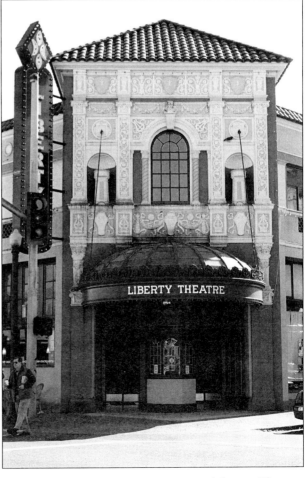

Liberty Theatre

Astoria

Points of Interest (continued)

- **Charles Stevens House**
  (*1388 Franklin*)
  Built in 1867.

- **Astoria Convent**
  (*14th and Franklin*)
  Built as the Rosebriar hotel in 1902, it is now a Bed and Breakfast.

- **St. Mary's Catholic Church**
  (*1465 Grand*)
  1902 construction. The first church was built in 1840.

- **Site of Old Fort Astoria**
  (*15th and Exchange*)
  The original fort would have taken up two city blocks.

- **Captain John Lawler House**
  (*1583 Franklin*)
  1868.

- **Site of First Post Office**
  (*15th between Franklin and Exchange*)
  This area is now occupied by the city hall. At the southeast corner of the hall is a stone slab that marks the grave of D. McTavish, a fur trader, who drowned in 1814. A partial replica of the fort is located here.

- **Astoria Pioneer Cemetery**
  (*15th and Madison*)
  Dates to 1835 and is one of the oldest cemeteries in the northwest.

- **Rose River Inn** (*1510 Franklin*)
  Another old home that has been converted to a B&B.

- **Grace Episcopal Church**
  (*1545 Franklin*)
  Dates to 1886.

- **Astoria Masonic Lodge #2**
  (*1572 Franklin*)
  A beautiful, old building.

- **Astor Column**
  (*15th to Coxcomb Hill*)
  Built in 1926, the column rises 125 feet and with 164 steps to the top, affords a panoramic view of the city, river, ocean, and the mountains.

Astoria Masonic Lodge

Site of Old Fort Astoria

- **Original Settlement Site**
  (16th and Exchange)
  The first post office west of the Rockies once stood here.

- **Heritage Museum**
  (1615 Exchange)
  Originally built in 1904 as the Astoria City Hall.

- **Brenham Van Duesen House**
  (1681 Franklin)
  Constructed in 1870.

- **Martin Foard House** *(690 17th)*
  This 1892 home is also a B&B.

- **Columbia River Maritime Museum** *(17th and Marine)*
  Features maritime relics and historical displays about Astoria and Clatsop County.

- **Astoria Train Station**
  (20th and Marine)
  An old, brick structure located on the waterfront Trolley Line.

- **Uppertown Firefighters Museum** *(30th and Marine)*
  Describes the history of fire fighting and fire fighting methods, and contains information about the tragic Astoria fires. The museum is housed in an 1896 brewery.

- **Astoria Inn** *(3391 Irving)*
  Another one-hundred year-old home converted to a B&B.

- **Benjamin Young House**
  (3652 Duane)
  This 1888 home of a sea captain is also a B&B.

Astor Column

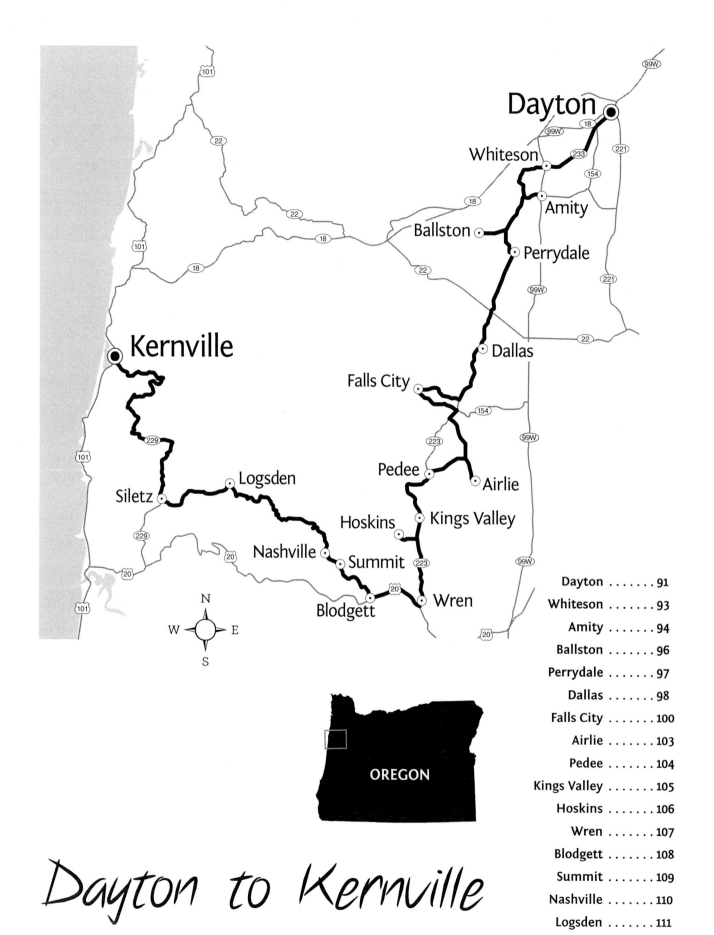

Dayton

99W

18

Whiteson

99W 233 221

Amity 154

18

Ballston

Perrydale 221

22

99W

22

Dallas

Falls City

154

Kernville 99W

223

229 Pedee Airlie

Logsden Kings Valley

Siletz Hoskins

229 Nashville Summit 223 99W

20 20

20 Blodgett Wren

101

N

W E

S

20

OREGON

Dayton 91
Whiteson 93
Amity 94
Ballston 96
Perrydale 97
Dallas 98
Falls City 100
Airlie 103
Pedee 104
Kings Valley 105
Hoskins 106
Wren 107
Blodgett 108
Summit 109
Nashville 110
Logsden 111
Siletz 112
Kernville 114

Dayton to Kernville

How Green is Kings Valley?

Dayton to Kernville (135 miles)

A glimpse of Oregon, unfamiliar to many travelers, can be seen along roads less traveled from
the community of Dayton, on the Yamhill River,
over the Coast Range Mountains to the Pacific
Ocean. Few other places in the United States
can offer a day trip like this one, which traverses
valley floor, freshwater wetlands, coastal rain
forest, and a marine estuary in one day. Sites of
interest along the way include covered bridges,
historic homes, various museums, a military
fort, and a wildlife refuge.

road less traveled near Kings Valley

Dayton

Elevation: 155 feet

Location:
45.13.240 N • 123.04.579

Services:
gas, food lodging, B&B

Dayton was platted during the winter of 1848-1849 by Joel Palmer, who helped Samuel K. Barlow blaze the Barlow Road, and Palmer's son-in-law, Andrew Smith. The town is situated on the Yamhill River, an important artery for early pioneer travel and commerce. Steamboats provided transportation beginning in 1851 and the Oregon Railway and Navigation Company maintained regular service for many years. The town was named for Dayton, Ohio, the former home of Smith. Palmer and Smith founded the community in 1850 and its post office was established in 1851. Dayton incorporated in 1880. Palmer was an Indiana Legislator before coming to Oregon, where he served as Superintendent of Indian Affairs. He was Speaker of the Oregon House in 1862 and State Senator from 1864-1866. Palmer lost the election for governor in 1870. Smith owned and operated a ferry that crossed the Yamhill River near Palmer Creek. Because of the location near the river, Dayton and the surrounding area were prone to flooding. In 1861, a devastating flood washed away businesses, docks and warehouses. Many merchants and farmers went bankrupt and the town eventually was rebuilt farther up the hill above the river. Subsequent floods continued to wipe out bridges and railroad tracks until river traffic, railroad traffic and general industry moved out of Dayton. A major fire hit the downtown in 1906. Dayton was the first city in Oregon designated as a national historic resource and has preserved many historic buildings, churches, and homes. Dayton centennial books and walking tour brochures are available at City Hall. Several wineries are located with minutes of the community. The area's economy is primarily dependent upon agriculture.

Fort Yamhill Blockhouse

Points of Interest

- **Fort Yamhill Blockhouse**
  (Court House Square)
  Constructed in 1855 and moved from Fort Hill in Grande Ronde to this site in the 1911.

- **Baptist Church** *(301 Main)*
  One of the oldest brick buildings in Yamhill County, built in 1886.

- **Nichols House** *(303 Main)*
  Constructed in 1895.

- **Londerhausen House**
  (309 Main)
  Built by hop grower and city councilman Paul Londerhausen in 1889.

- **US Bank** *(302 Ferry)*
  This former drugstore with the IOOF Lodge upstairs was constructed in 1913.

- **Stuckey Building** *(304 Ferry)*
  Divided into two sections that contained a grocery store, post office, printing office and a mercantile store.

- **Dayton Post Office** (*308 Ferry*) Originally the 1910 Oregon Mutual Merchant Fire Insurance Association. Became the post office in 1915.

- **Fisher Butcher Shop** (*400 Ferry*) The meat market opened in 1918.

- **Samuel Sigler House** (*521 Ferry*) Sigler, a lumberman, built this house in 1904.

- **Dayton Common School** (*506 4th*) Built in 1860 and now a private residence.

- **Evangelical United Brethren Church** (*302 5th*) Constructed between 1883 and 1887.

- **John Baxter House** (*407 Church*) Baxter, who is buried in Brookside Cemetery, built this home in 1890.

- **Mellinger House** (*414 5th*) Built in 1904 for real estate developer James Mellinger.

- **Hibbert Residence** (*426 5th*) Herman Wilson built this for his bride in 1906; the marriage fell through and he never lived in the home.

- **Rippey House** (*523 Ash*) Built around 1890.

Joel Palmer House

Andrew Smith House II

- **Joel Palmer House** (*600 Ferry*) Joel Palmer built this home in 1857. It is now a restaurant.

- **Gabriel-Will House** (*401 3rd*) Built in 1885 by Christopher and Sarah Taylor.

- **Brookside Cemetery** (*3rd and Mill*) Joel Palmer established the cemetery in the 1850s.

- **Methodist Church Parsonage** (*202 4th*) Built around 1868.

- **Dayton Methodist Episcopal Church** (*302 4th*) Opened in 1862 and was the first church in Dayton.

- **Robert Morris House** (*409 Oak*) Constructed in the late 1870s and once sold at sheriff's auction for $6.00.

- **Free Methodist Church** (*411 Oak*) Known as Dayton's third church, this building was constructed in 1885.

- **Carter House** (*521 Church*) Constructed in 1908 and later owned by the town dentist.

- **Andrew Smith House II** (*308 5th*) The second home of the town co-founder was built in 1859.

- **Goodrich House** (*324 6th*) Built in the 1890s and residence of the town doctor.

- **Shippy House** (*421 6th*) 1891 construction. Shippy was a dry goods merchant.

- **Mabee House** (*309 7th*) Contractor Emerson Mabee built this home in 1889.

- **Henry Bertram Sr. House** (*6160 SE Webfoot Road*) 1892.

Dayton to Whiteson

Distance:
7.6 miles

Directions:
Drive west on Ferry (Highway 233) toward Whiteson.

Points En Route

(mileage from 4th and Ferry)

0.6 miles:
A once grand house.

0.8 miles:
Ferry Street becomes Highway 233.

1.6 miles:
Intersection. Stay on Highway 233.

2.1 miles:
Keep left on Highway 223.

2.3 miles:
Stringtown Road.

5.6 miles:
Eola Village. A flourishing 1950s and 1960s migrant labor camp.

6.7 miles:
Turn right on Whiteson Road.

7.6 miles:
Whiteson

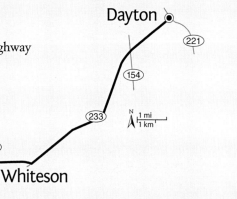

Whiteson

Elevation: 164 feet

Location:
45.09.601 N • 123.11.709 W

Services:
none

Whiteson was named for Henry White, who platted the town and donated the right-of-way for the narrow gauge railroad that ran through Whiteson and linked Portland and Airlie. Even though locals called their community White and the post office established as Whites in 1889, the railroad used Whiteson, a name officially adopted in 1890. Whiteson was settled as an Amish community, and had close ties with nearby Amity. The first school opened in 1892 and closed in 1936 when students were transported to Amity. Whiteson, larger than McMinnville at the time, was considered to become the Yamhill County Seat. Lack of water terminated consideration.

Points of Interest

- **Taylor (Whiteson) Cemetery**
  (on Telegraph Hill off of Highway 233)
  At 6320 Telegraph, travel about 0.1 mile up the hill to the 1850s Taylor (Whiteson) Cemetery.

Taylor (Whiteson) Cemetery

Whiteson to Amity

Distance:
6.3 miles

Directions:
From the intersection of Whiteson Road and Highway 99, cross Highway 99 and the railroad tracks, traveling on River Bend Road.

Points En Route

(mileage from the intersection of Whiteson Road and Highway 99)

0.4 miles:
8910 River Bend Road. Old home and barn.

1.5 miles:
Intersection with Hook and Eye Lane. Keep right on River Bend Road. The name Hook and Eye Lane reflects Amish influence by settlers in the area.

2.1 miles:
Intersection of River Bend Road and Briedwell Lane. Go left on Briedwell.

2.7 miles:
Victorian house and barn.

3.2 miles:
Sheldon Farms.

4.0 miles:
Picturesque barns.

4.8 miles:
Crossing railroad tracks.

4.9 miles:
At the intersection of Briedwell Lane and Bellevue Highway, turn left on Bellevue Highway and travel toward Amity. At the north end of this intersection is the 1895 Briedwell School, 11935 SW Bellevue Highway, now a private residence.

6.2 miles:
Crossing Salt Creek.

6.3 miles:
Amity

Amity

Elevation: 162 feet

Location:
45.11.543 N • 123.20.632 W

Services:
gas, food

Brothers Joseph and Ahio Watt first settled in the area in 1848. This former Willamette Valley hub for prune and dairy farming was once an Amish community, yet it was named not for its inhabitants but as a result of an 'amicable settlement' between two schools disputing over land. Ahio Watt was the first schoolteacher and the name Amity was first applied to the community's school in 1849. The post office was established in 1852 and Joseph Watt constructed a flourmill in the late 1850s, sending flour round Cape Horn in 1868. Watt also built Oregon's first woolen mill in Amity and the railroad arrived in 1879, ending passenger service in 1939. Amity incorporated in 1880 and the first newspaper in Amity, called the *Amity Popgun*, was printed in 1892. The first bank opened in 1905, about the same time that electricity was made available. In the early days, Amity was home to several banks, hotels, and a Chinese laundry. The majority of its Amish citizenry returned to the east in the 1940s. Modern Amity and the surrounding area boasts wineries and vineyards, historic churches and homes, antique stores, nurseries and farms.

Points of Interest

- **Amity Middle School**
  (Church and Getchell)
  Occupies the land where the 1853 Methodist Church once stood.

- **Christian Church**
  (Getchell and Maddox)
  Constructed in 1875.

Barn in Amity

Amity

Points of Interest (continued)

- **Brown House** (*Oak and Nursery*) 1887 construction.

- **Amity Methodist Church** (*203 Nursery*)
  The church was established here in 1846 and the building constructed in 1892.

- **Victorian House** (*304 Nursery*)
  One of Amity's grander homes complete with wrought iron fence.

- **Masonic Lodge and Amity Furniture Store** (*418 Trade*)
  Lodge meetings were held upstairs. The furniture store gave way to Schulmerich's Mercantile.

- **Amity Cemetery** (*5th and Woodland*)
  Dates to 1854.

- **Amity Bank** (*502 Trade*)
  Opened in the early 1920s.

- **Ranchers Market** (*504 Trade*)
  This 1855 building was moved to this site and served as Amity's first school.

- **Cronk Building** (*506-510 Trade*)
  Circa 1909.

- **IOOF Building** (*514-518 Trade*)
  Built in 1912, a drug store occupied the first floor and the upstairs was the meeting hall for the Odd Fellows.

- **Doctor's Office** (*602 Trade*)
  Home and office of the doctor.

- **First Baptist Church** (*205 6th*)
  The oldest surviving church in Amity was built in 1858.

- **Ahio Watt House** (*311 6th*)
  The town co-founder built this home in the 1860s.

- **Buffam Stage House** (*6th and Trade*)
  The old stage stop was built in 1875.

- **Old House** (*1002 Oak*)
  Beautiful stained glass windows.

- **Boyd House** (*1303 Goucher*)
  Built in 1875.

- **Amity Vineyard and Winery** (*18150 SE Amity Vineyard Road*)
  Take Rice Lane to SE Amity Vineyard Road.

IOOF Building

Ahio Watt House

Ballston

Elevation: 162 feet

Location:
43.04.004 N • 123.19.164 W

Services:
none

Ballston was named for Isaac Ball, who, in 1850, took his donation land claim where the community now stands. The post office was originally established as Ballsville in 1878 but the name was changed to Ballston in 1880. Ballston was an important stop on the Dayton, Sheridan and Grande Ronde Railway, which later became the Oregonian Railroad Company. Relatives of Daniel Boone were early settlers here. In 1915, Ballston boasted a public school, two churches and three fraternal organizations. Today, two old schoolhouses, a block apart, form the core of this small community. The old grocery store, converted to an antique store, closed many years ago. Salt Creek, which flows through town, received its name from the saltlicks that farmer's placed near the banks of this creek. The 1928 Salt Creek Church stands several miles away. Today, as in the past, Ballston is a farming community.

Amity to Ballston

Distance:
7.5 miles

Directions:
At Trade and 5th, turn right on 5th and drive west. 5th Street becomes the Bellevue Highway.

Points En Route

(mileage from the intersection of Trade and 5th)

0.3 miles:
Crossing Salt Creek.

1.6 miles:
Crossing railroad tracks.

2.2 miles:
Turn left and travel on Broadmead Road.

3.4 miles:
The 1976 Brigittine Monastery. Stems from the 1370 Swedish Order and is famous for its gourmet fudge and other confections which can be sampled in the gift store.

5.1 miles:
Site of Broadmead, which had its own post office in 1915. *Broadmead* is Anglo-Saxon for "Broad Meadow."

6.6 miles:
Victorian Farmhouse.

7.5 miles:
Ballston

Points of Interest

Lawn Arbor School

- **Lawn Arbor School**
  (Ballston Road)
  Built from local lumber and square nails, this 1855 school, which is furnished with desks, chairs, books, and a potbelly stove, was moved two miles west from its original location. The school was used until 1875. The accompanying outhouse was also moved to this location.

- **Ballston Grocery** *(intersection of Ballston Road and De Jong Road)*
  Long closed.

- **Old Ballston School** *(one block south of the old grocery store)*
  Operated as a private, charter school.

Ballston to Perrydale

Distance:
4.8 miles

Directions:
Double back on Ballston Road toward Broadmead.

Points En Route

(mileage from the intersection of Ballston Road and De Jong Road)

1.3 miles:
Intersection with Tucker Road. This is the site of Tucker, once an important railroad terminal on the Dayton, Sheridan and Grande Ronde Railway. Continue straight on Ballston Road.

2.3 miles:
Turn right on Broadmead Road.

4.6 miles:
Turn left on West Perrydale Road.

4.8 miles:
Perrydale

Ballston

N 2000 ft / 500 m

Perrydale

Perrydale

Elevation: 175 feet

Location:
45.02.531 N • 123.15.308 W

Services:
none

Perrydale, a tiny, bucolic, unincorporated, farming community speckled with Victorian-era homes, a school and small fabrication plant, was named after William Perry, a pioneer landowner. The post office was established in 1870 and closed in 1971. An Oregonian Railway Company station was established here in 1881. In 2006, the old train depot was moved to the Douglas County Train Depot Museum near Roseburg. A handful of homes and buildings line the semi-circular Perrydale Loop Drive where a flourmill, church and general store once prospered. Residents work as farmers and loggers or commute to jobs in nearby communities.

Old house near Perrydale

Points of Interest

- **Perrydale Loop Drive**
  (downtown Perrydale)
  Barns, garages, an old warehouse, the location of the old train depot, and several old houses on a graveled four-block loop. This was once the residential hub of the community.

- **Old Gas Station and Garage**
  (corner of Perrydale and West Perrydale Roads)
  An antique steam tractor rests in front of the building.

- **Seed Cleaning Warehouse**
  (on Perrydale Loop)
  Consists of several buildings.

Distance:
7.7 miles

Directions:
From the intersection with West Perrydale Road, travel south on Perrydale Road toward Dallas.

Points En Route

(mileage from the intersection of Perrydale Road and West Perrydale Road)

0.1 miles:
The Perrydale Baptist Church, 7450 Perrydale Road, was constructed in 1885.

0.2 miles:
Beautiful, grand, Victorian era home and landscaped yard (7355 Perrydale Road).

1.1 miles:
Old German Baptist Church Road. The old church is seven miles off the road.

5.9 miles:
Dolph Corner. Once a small settlement, now a busy highway intersection. Cross highway 22 continuing south on Perrydale Road. The Baskett Slough National Wildlife Refuge lies 2.0 miles southeast of the intersection on Highway 22.

7.7 miles:
Dallas

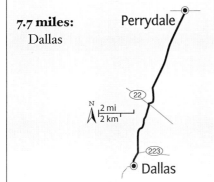

Dallas

Elevation: 325 feet

Location:
44.55.163 N • 123.18.583 W

Services:
gas, food, lodging, B&B

Originally called Cynthia Ann, the town was settled in 1844 on the north side of Rickreall Creek. Two stories offer different explanations for the naming of this newly formed community. One story says that "Cynthiana" was the name chosen by Mrs. Thomas Lovelady, early resident, in loving memory of her home in Kentucky. The second story says the name was chosen to honor "Cynthia Ann," the wife of resident Jesse Applegate. Regardless, an inadequate water supply forced the town to move more than one mile south in 1856 and the name was changed in honor of George Mifflin Dallas, vice-president of the United States from 1845 to 1849. Dallas served under President James K. Polk, for which Polk County was named. The Dallas post office opened in 1852. The town incorporated in 1874 and the railroad came to town in 1878, which helped Dallas win control of county government over rival Independence. Louis Gerlinger incorporated the Salem, Falls City and Western Railway Company in October of 1901. In 1903 the first train ran from Dallas to Falls City, and began making regular daily stops. Gerlinger founded Willamette Industries in 1906, and the lumber company operated continuously until 2002. Dallas, Polk County Seat, was once known as "Prune City, USA." Dallas had an active KKK chapter in the 1920s. Rickreall Creek, the name derived from *hyak chuck* – Chinook for 'swift water' - runs through the community and it's large City Park where Summerfest is held in July.

*Polk County
Courthouse*

Points of Interest

- **Dallas City Park** (*new section at 401 SW Levens Street; old section at 600 SW Allgood Street*)
A thirty-five acre park, the largest of several maintained by the city. The Delbert Hunter Arboretum and Botanic Garden is situated at the south end and a bridge from the Brandvold section of the park leads to the Japanese Garden. The park features playground areas, horseshoe pits, basketball hoops, disc golf course, fireplaces, BBQ pits, picnic tables, a kitchen, two fireplaces, several sinks, restrooms, shelters and a swimming hole in the creek.

Dallas

Points of Interest (continued)

- **La Creole Academy**
  (182 Academy)
  Began operations in 1857 and merged with Dallas College in 1900, offering bachelor's degrees until 1914, when lack of funds deemed the academy substandard. The building served as Dallas High School from 1929-1954.

- **Dallas Carnegie Library**
  (187 Court)
  The old library building was constructed in the early 1900s and was moved to 950 Main.

- **Gail Hotel** *(880 Church)*
  Rates are posted on the windows: $10 a day and $100 a month.

- **Majestic Theater** *(976 Main)*
  The old theater is now an event center.

- **Polk County Courthouse**
  (800 Main)
  Constructed with locally quarried sandstone in 1898 to replace a previous wooden structure burned in an arson fire. The hanging tree, used for executions (it stood south of the original courthouse), was cut down when an addition was made to the old building.

- **Dallas Drive-In Theater**
  (315 Fir Villa Road)
  The drive-in, continuously operating since 1953, is Oregon's largest outdoor movie screen.

- **Basket Slough** *(north and east of town on Highway 22)*
  The refuge and sanctuary covers almost 2500 acres of land. Bald eagles winter on the refuge and over 200 other bird species, thirty species of mammals, ten species of reptiles, and eight species of amphibians have been identified. The largest population of the rare Fender Blue Butterfly can be found here.

- **Polk County Museum**
  (Highway 99 in Rickreall)
  An excellent museum and worth the six-mile drive.

- **Site of Ellendale**
  (west on Ellendale Road)
  James O'Neal, who built a gristmill here in 1844, settled this former community. Ellendale had its own post office in 1850 and sawmill in 1854. Slave quarters were constructed here by one of the mill owners about the time of the Civil War. The iron bars, used to imprison the slaves, are displayed in the Polk County Museum.

- **Orchard View School**
  (775 Ellendale Road)
  A two-room oldie moved to this location from the former community of Ellendale to the west.

Dallas Carnegie Library

Home in Dallas

Dallas to Falls City

Distance:
9.1 miles

Directions:
From the stoplight at South Main and Washington (Highway 223), turn on Washington (Highway 223) and drive south. This road follows the 1848 Applegate Trail.

Points En Route

(mileage from the traffic light at South Main and Washington)

1.1 miles:
The 1847 Dallas Cemetery.

2.4 miles:
Applegate Trail marker.

3.9 miles:
Guthrie Park and the old Guthrie School gymnasium. Guthrie, a coffin maker who came to Oregon in 1846, built his home near this intersection. The last coffin he made, before settling in the area, was for his wife.

5.4 miles:
Falls City turn-off. Turn right and proceed west on Falls City Road.

8.7 miles:
Odd Fellows Cemetery - on the left.

8.7 miles:
Falls City Cemetery and Anderson Cemetery - on the right. The Anderson family cemetery and gravesites are adjacent to the Falls City Cemetery.

9.1 miles:
Falls City

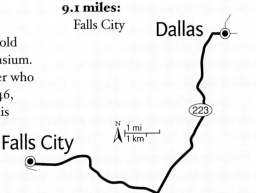

Bridge Park

Falls City

Elevation: 365 feet

Location:
44.51.555 N • 123.26.191 W

Services:
gas, food, RV

Named for the falls at the west edge of town, Falls City was once known as the "Queen City of Polk County." Osborne Russell staked the first land claim in 1845, which included the land around the falls. Thorp took over his claim and built a sawmill in 1852 and a gristmill in 1853. At its peak, the community was home to fifteen sawmills, five churches, several grocery stores, taverns and barbershops, a shoe store, confectionery, jewelry store, butcher shop, bakery, blacksmith, and offices for a doctor, dentist and a newspaper. There once existed a hospital, hotel, bank and cannery, as well as a livery stable, skating rink, and hydroelectric plant. The Falls City post office opened in 1889, and the community was first charted in 1893 and officially recognized as a city in 1903, the same year the Dallas-Falls City train began operating. The entire community was negatively affected with the decline of the lumber industry, which ended completely when the last mill burned to the ground in 1965. This sleepy community of less than 1,000 residents has four city parks. Falls City is a gateway to the spectacular BLM Old Growth timber preserve and famed Valley of the Giants in the Coast Range Mountains.

Points of Interest

- **Falls City High School**
  (111 N Main)
  Built in 1904.

- **Falls City Elementary**
  (177 Prospect)
  High on the hill above town.

100

Falls City

Points of Interest (continued)

- **Falls City United Methodist Church** (*1st and Main*)
Originally the Beulah Methodist-Episcopal Church, constructed in 1892.

- **Luckiwood House** (*180 Dayton*)
Near one of the footbridges that cross the river, this home was built in 1900.

- **Old Falls City Post Office** (*corner of 3rd and Main*)
Today a massage parlor.

- **Falls City Hall** (*299 Mill*)
Built in the 1920s, the old jail, with two cells, is attached to this building.

- **Luckiamute Falls** (*200 block of Parry*)
These are the falls for which the city is named. The city park affords an excellent view and has a great picnic area. Luckiamute refers to the Native American Indian Tribe who lived here.

- **George Kitchen Park** (*on Mitchell between 7th and Park*)
Also known as the Upper Park, with large gazebo and access to electricity.

- **Michael Harding Park** (*next to the Luckiamute Falls*)
First known as the New Upper Falls Park and dedicated in memory of a late city clerk.

- **Bridge Park** (*on Pine between 2nd and 3rd*)

- **Fay Wilson Memorial Park** (*parallels the river from Bridge Street to Dayton Street opposite City Hall*)
Also known as Riverside Park and the Lower Park.

- **Gerlinger County Park** (*3 miles west on the Little Luckiamute River via Black Rock Road*)
Access to the river for recreational activities.

- **Camp Kilowan** (*6510 Teal Creek Road*)
The Camp Fire Girls camp opened in the 1920s.

- **Camp Tapawingo** (*22505 Black Rock Road*)
Opened in 1953. The Baptist Church camp covers 160 acres in the Black Rock area. Tapawingo means "Joy of Spirit."

Falls City High School

Luckiwood House

Falls City to Airlie

Distance:

11.4 miles

Directions:

At downtown Falls City, go across the bridge (Bridge Street).

Points En Route

(mileage from the bridge)

0.1 miles:

Turn left on S Main Street.

0.2 miles:

Green Haven RV Park.

0.4 miles:

Turn left on Sheldon Street.

0.8 miles:

Sheldon becomes Bridgeport Road. Stay on Bridgeport Road.

1.0 miles:

Well-maintained gravel road.

2.0 miles:

Pavement returns.

2.5 miles:

Intersection with Gardner Road. Stay on Bridgeport Road.

3.0 miles:

Crossing the Luckiamute River.

3.0 miles:

Site of Bridgeport. The old school was constructed in the 1920s and is now the Luckiamute Charter School. The post office opened under the name of Bridge Port in 1854, soon changed its name to Bridgeport, and then closed in 1874.

3.0 miles:

Intersection with Liberty Road. Turn right, staying on Bridgeport Road.

3.6 miles:

Bridgeport Community Chapel, 16390 Bridgeport Road.

4.4 miles:

Intersection with Highway 223. Turn right.

5.3 miles:

Highway 223 and Airlie Road intersection. Turn left onto Airlie Road.

8.7 miles:

Old farmhouse.

9.4 miles:

Intersection with Maple Grove Road. Stay on Airlie Road.

11.2 miles:

Applegate Trail marker and Airlie Farm and B&B (14810 Airlie Road).

11.4 miles:

Airlie

Bridgeport School

Airlie

Elevation: 244 feet

Location:
44.45.073 N • 123.19.816 W

Services:
none

Airlie was platted in 1877 when local farmers joined forces to bring the narrow gauge line of the Oregon Railway Company to the area. The station was named for the Earl of Airlie of Scotland, president of the company, who visited Oregon during the course of the line's construction. In 1881, the terminus was completed at Airlie, along with several homes for railroad workers. The Airlie post office opened in 1882, shortly after the arrival of the train. At one time, Airlie had two merchandise stores, a train depot, meat market, school, church, and hop warehouse. All the tracks were removed by 1929. Local lumber mills added to the small local population and the economy before the logging boom ended. Today little remains but a few homes.

Former Church

Points of Interest

- **Site of Airlie Store**
  (*intersection of Airlie Road and Maxfield Creek Road*)
  The old store was the hub of the community, with its potbelly stove serving as a focal point for both warmth and conversation. All that remains today is a brick building that stood next to the false front store.

- **Former Church**
  (*14620 Airlie Road*)
  Converted to a home in the 1960s.

- **Site of Airlie School** (*14580 Airlie Road, next to the old church*)
  Nothing remains of the two-room, 1910 school.

- **Airlie Winery**
  (*west on Maxwell Creek Road*)
  Opened in 1986, approximately 3 miles from the intersection of Maxwell Creek Road and Airlie Road. The intersection is also the site of the old, false-front general store.

Airlie to Pedee

Distance:
6.0 miles

Directions:
Backtrack 1.9 miles on Airlie Road to Maple Grove Road.

Points En Route

(*mileage from the intersection of Maxwell Creek Road and Airlie Road*)

1.8 miles:
Crossing the Luckiamute River.

1.9 miles:
Intersection with Maple Grove Road; turn left.

2.0 miles:
Site of Maple Grove, which once consisted of a school, blacksmith shop, and general store, all of which have been torn down. Continue west on Maple Grove Road toward Pedee.

5.4 miles:
Intersection with Kings Valley Highway (highway 223). Turn left.

6.0 miles:
Pedee

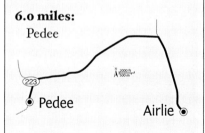

Pedee

Elevation: 267 feet

Location:
44.45.111 N • 123.24.501 W

Services:
food (if store is open)

Pedee gets its name from Colonel Cornelius Gilliam, who came to Oregon from North Carolina in 1844, and whose family named the local creek after a river back home. Gilliam was killed in a shooting accident during the Cayuse War of 1848 and Eastern Oregon's Gilliam County was named in his honor. (Gilliam is pronounce Gil – um) The Pedee post office opened in 1919 and the old school, converted to a residence, was built in 1924.

Points of Interest

- **Pedee Blue Jeans Factory**
  (*11155 Kings Valley Highway*)
  In operation since 1983.

- **Pedee Women's Club**
  (*12491 Kings Valley Highway*)
  Used for multiple purposes.

- **Pedee Memorial Evangelical Church**
  (*12975 King Valley Highway*)

- **Pedee Store (18785 Depot)**
  The old store has been converted to a home.

- **Pedee Cemetery**
  (*Ira Hooker Road*)
  Dates to the 1860s.

Pedee Women's Club

Pedee to Kings Valley

Distance:
5.0 miles

Directions:
Continue west on Kings Valley Highway (Highway 223).

Points En Route

(mileage from the Pedee Store)

0.3 miles:
Old mill site. One of many in the area that once operated twenty-four hours every day.

1.4 miles:
Pedee Creek.

1.7 miles:
Old Pedee School, converted to a private residence (12975 Kings Valley Highway).

1.8 miles:
Pedee Memorial Church (12995 Kings Valley Highway).

3.5 miles:
Rittner Creek Covered

Bridge and Rittner Rutter Wayside Park. The bridge is currently open to foot traffic and picnicking. The bridge was named for Sebastian Rittner, an 1854 pioneer, and cost was $7,000 to construct in 1926 and $26,000 to move in 1974. The former community of Rittner was located nearby.

4.0 miles:
Entering Benton County.

5.0 miles:
Kings Valley

Rittner Creek Covered Bridge

Kings Valley

Elevation: 327 feet

Location:
43.42.338 N • 123.42.324 W

Services:
gas, food

Kings Valley was named for Nahum King, an 1845 pioneer settler in the area, and a survivor of the ill-fated wagon train that followed Stephen Meek on his supposed short cut from Boise to the Willamette Valley. King's daughter Sarah died along the way, but fifteen of his other children survived the arduous journey. The Kings built a flourmill here in 1853, one of the first in the state. The town's post office was established in 1855, with Rowland Chambers, King's son-in-law and Sarah's widower, serving as postmaster. The office closed in 1974. Skeletal remains of what was once one of the largest mills in Polk County lie to the left of the entrance to the community. Even though Kings Valley was officially platted, evidence of the streets is no longer visible and the town never incorporated. The Valley and Siletz Railroad used to make daily runs through the community.

Points of Interest

- **Kings Valley Store**
  (39088 Kings Valley Highway)
  This is the third store on the site. The first burned in 1914 and the second in 1985. An old photo, inside the store, shows the original store and nearby homes.

- **Former Mill**
  (site of old mill)
  Very little evidence is left of the many mills that once dotted this area.

Mill Remains

Kings Valley to Hoskins

Distance:
  3.5 miles

Directions:
  Proceed south on the Kings Valley Highway (Highway 223).

Points En Route

(mileage from the Kings Valley Store)

0.1 miles:
  An old home with a commemorative marker – Rowland Chambers and Nahum King, 1846.

0.3 miles:
  Kings Valley Church, more than 100 years old.

0.4 miles:
  Kings Valley School. The district was established in 1848 and is open today as a charter school.

0.6 miles:
  Approximate site of the Nahum King homestead, torn down in 1999.

1.6 miles:
  The 1848 Kings Valley Cemetery. King is buried here.

1.8 miles:
  Turn right on Hoskins Summit Road, which is also called Luckiamute Road.

2.6 miles:
  Bush family Century Farm.

3.1 miles:
  Three houses (on the right side of the road) whose back doors and porches face the paved road. The homes were constructed to face the original 1850s Fort Hoskins Military Road.

3.5 miles:
  Intersection of Hoskins Road and Luckiamute Road.

3.5 miles:
  Hoskins

Hoskins

Elevation: 336 feet

Location:
43.40.437 N • 123.28.303 W

Services:
none

Little remains as evidence of the activity that existed here in the 1850s, when Fort Hoskins was built and fortified under the supervision of Lt. Phil Sheridan. The fort was named for an officer killed in the battle of Monterey during the Mexican War, and its purpose was to prevent Native Americans from harming the valley's settlers. The town that grew up near the fort later became an important agricultural and lumber terminus for the railroad.

Fort Hoskins County Park

Points of Interest

- **Site of Old Fort Tavern**
  The last business to close (2000) in this small community stood in the clearing near the split rail fence. It was torn down in 2008.

- **Site of Watson House**
  (near the creek as the road turns toward the park)
  This was designed to be the finest house west of Salem. A covered bridge used to span the creek where the new bridge now stands. An interpretive walk passes by the site of the old house, which burned in 1990.

- **Fort Hoskins County Park**
  (top of hill)
  The site of Fort Hoskins and the town of Hoskins, once located on a major territorial road connecting the coast with the valley, comprise one of Benton County's newest parks. From 1856 to 1865 as many as three hundred men were stationed here. Their job was to patrol the Coast Indian Reservation, home to the Luckiamute band of the Kalapuya Tribe, and to ward off conflict between the Native Americans and encroaching settlers. A bloodless insurrection by Native Americans near Yaquina Bay was squelched. The Hoskins General Store, which stood near the railroad tracks and the creek, closed in 1963 and was torn down the same year. The railroad ceased operating in 1978.

Hoskins to Wren

Distance:
7.7 miles

Directions:
Backtrack 1.7 miles, returning to Kings Valley Highway (Highway 223).

Points En Route

(mileage from the bridge)

1.7 miles:
Turn right on Kings Valley Highway (Highway 223).

3.2 miles:
Beazell Memorial Forest. The Fender Blue butterfly can be spotted here.

6.7 miles:
Wren Community Hall (35535 Highway 223 near Cardwell Hill Drive). Built in 1939 and center of community activity.

6.8 miles:
Cardwell Cellars.

7.7 miles:
Wren

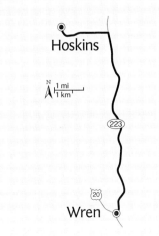

Wren

Elevation: 629 feet

Location:
44.35.264 N • 123.25.600 W

Services:
gas, food

Several pioneer families settled in this area in the 1850s, but it was not until the railroad came through here in 1886, opening the area to logging, that the community began to grow. The Wren post office opened in 1887 and a small community was built around the mills. When the timber industry died, the post office closed in 1968. During the peak of the timber industry, numerous mills stood within a fifteen-mile radius of Wren, which was named for an early Benton County pioneer George Wren. Today, skeletons of those mills serve as a reminder of logging's impact on the area, though only a few houses remain in this once prosperous community.

Wren Railroad Depot

Wren to Blodgett

Distance:
4.9 miles

Directions:
From the intersection of Highway 223 and Highway 20, turn right and travel west on Highway 20.

Points En Route

(mileage from the intersection of Highway 223 and Highway 20)

4.5 miles:
Crossing Norton Creek, named for a pioneer family.

4.9 miles:
Blodgett

Points of Interest

- **Wren Railroad Depot**
  (next to the tracks)
  The depot is now a small business office.

- **Harris Covered Bridge**
  (2.5 miles on Rittner Road)
  This bridge, built in 1936 to connect the people of Harris and Wren with the mills, is the third to span Mary's River at this point.

Harris Covered Bridge

Blodgett

Elevation: 591 feet

Location:
44.35.514 N • 123.31.713 W

Services:
gas, food

Blodgett is located on the banks of the Mary's River near the confluence with the Tum Tum River. The community's first post office opened in 1888 under the name of Emerick after a local pioneer family. The name was changed to Blodgett, one month later, to honor William Blodgett, also a pioneer resident. The post office is still located in the general store, which was constructed the same year. Several lumber mills dotted the area, the largest existing across the street from the store. Photos of the mill can be viewed inside the old store.

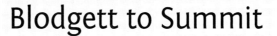
Blodgett Country Store

Points of Interest

- **Blodgett Country Store**
  (21412 Highway 20)
  Constructed and in operation since 1888. Old photos line the walls of the store.

- **Blodgett School**
  (35177 Tum Tum Road)
  Built in 1929 and today serves about twenty-five primary grade students. The first school in Blodgett was built in 1850.

Blodgett to Summit

Distance:
4.6 miles

Directions:
From the store, cross Highway 20, taking the Summit-Nashville Road. The road will climb more than 500 feet in the last two miles before reaching Summit.

Points En Route

(mileage from the intersection of Highway 20 and Summit-Nashville Road)

3.9 miles:
Summit Cemetery.

4.6 miles:
Summit

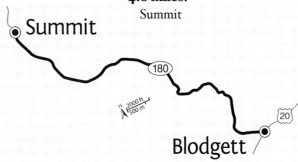

Summit

Elevation: 591 feet

Location:
44.38.161 N • 123.34.342 W

Services:
none

Located at the crest of the watersheds between the Willamette Valley to the east and the Yaquina River to the west, Summit is appropriately named. At one time, this unincorporated community was called Summitville.

Points of Interest

- **Summit General Store**
  (*19904 Summit Highway*)
  Constructed in 1889 and recently converted to a private residence and a musical instrument maker's studio.

- **Summit Community Center**
  (*19891 Summit Highway*)
  An old church, moved to this location, serves as the center of community activity.

- **Summit Grange #432**
  (*19883 Summit Highway*)
  This grange, located near the railroad tracks, is almost 100 years old.

- **Summit House of Ill Repute**
  (*directly across the tracks from the community center*)
  This former bordello, with several small rooms on its second floor, is now a private residence.

Summit General Store

Summit Community Center

Summit to Nashville

Distance:
2.3 miles

Directions:
Proceed west on the Summit-Nashville Road. This route drops more than five hundred feet in elevation. Mosses and lichens cover much of the forest canopy.

Points En Route

(*mileage from the old general store*)

0.5 miles:
Single-lane trestle underpass.

1.4 miles:
Entering Lincoln County.

2.3 miles:
Nashville

Nashville

Elevation: 239 feet

Location:
44.39.121 N • 123.26.341 W

Services:
none

Lincoln County's Nashville was named for Wallis Nash, a native of England who settled in Oregon in 1879 and was involved in various enterprises, including the construction of the railroad between Corvallis and Yaquina Bay. Wallis, a successful lawyer, lived in Nashville for many years.

Points of Interest

- **Old Gas Station and General Store** (*12060 Nashville Road*)
  One of the few remaining structural holdouts in the former community, this building has been converted to a second hand store and food bank.

Old Gas Station and General Store

Nashville to Logsden

Distance:
14.2 miles

Directions:
From the intersection of Nashville Road and Logsden Road (Highway 411), turn right and travel on Logsden Road toward Siletz.

Points En Route

(mileage from the Summit-Nashville and Highway 411 intersection)

2.4 miles:
Pavement ends.

4.1 miles:
Pavement returns at Hammar Lake, a man-made reservoir.

8.9 miles:
Llhuuke Illahee Fish Hatchery, operated by the Siletz Indians.

10.5 miles:
Three 'itchin' posts, planted in the ground for pastured animals.

14.1 miles:
Logsden Community Club.

14.2 miles:
Logsden

110

Logsden

Elevation: 195 feet

Location:
44.34.323 N • 123.47.452 W

Services:
gas, food

Logsden was named to honor a prominent member of the Siletz Tribe who lived in the area. The post office was first established in 1914 as Orton, the name of a local family, then changed to Logsden in 1921. Not much has changed in Logsden in many years, although the pace is slower because only a few log trucks rumble down the highway. The general store is still the center of the community.

Points of Interest

- **Logsden Community Center**
  (6966 Logsden Road)
  Next to the river, circa 1960.
  Playground.

- **Logsden Country Store**
  (7550 Logsden Road)
  Serving locals, hunters, anglers, loggers and visitors. This 1968 building replaced the old store that stood near the river.

- **Moonshine Park**
  (Moonshine Park Road)
  Named for the illegal moonshine activity that occurred long ago.

Logsden Country Store

Logsden to Siletz

Distance:
9.5 miles

Directions:
From the store, continue west on Highway 411 (Logsden Road).

Points En Route

(mileage from the store)

0.9 miles:
Logsden Neighborhood Church.

2.7 miles:
Sam's Creek Road. Nearby is Twin Bridges Memorial Park, with a picnic area, rest rooms, and boat launch. The new, concrete bridge replaced the 1922 Sam's Creek Covered Bridge.

5.3 miles:
Riverside Cemetery (VFW).

9.5 miles:
Government Point, established in 1885, serves as the center of government for the Confederated Tribes of the Siletz. A quarter-mile drive or walk takes you to the top. The grounds are beautifully maintained and include a tribal cemetery (these are sacred grounds; inquire before entering). At one time, the reservation stretched from Tillamook to Yachats, but was later reduced to about 40,000 acres.

9.5 miles:
Siletz

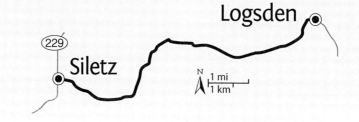

Siletz

Elevation: 130 feet

Location:
44.43.181 N • 123.55.122 W

Services:
gas, food

The Siletz Indians are the southern-most Salishan Tribe on the Oregon Coast. The name now designates all the tribes on the Siletz Reservation, which includes members of the Athapascan, Kusan, Takilman, Shastan, Shahaptian, and Yakonan linguistic families. Siletz has been spelled and pronounced several ways, including Celeste, Neselitch, and Sailets, coming from the French word *celeste*, meaning 'heavenly.' The town of Siletz is a unique mixture of old and new, with older homes being the rule. There is a sense that life is less hectic here than elsewhere and time seems to be greatly respected. The community incorporated in 1946. The Siletz Brewery closed in 2009 when it moved to Albany.

Siletz Valley School

Points of Interest

- **Siletz Tribal Offices**
  (565 Old River Road)
  A beautifully crafted building.

- **Siletz Grange #558** *(215 Gaither)*
  The old building is available for private functions.

- **Siletz Valley School**
  (245 James Frank)
  Now open as a charter school.

- **Siletz City Hall** *(215 W Buford)*
  Dates to 1946.

- **Old Mill Site Park**
  (NE Mill Park Drive)
  Boat launch.

- **Hee Hee Illahee Park** *(corner of Highway 214 and S Gaither)*
  Boat launch and parking area.

- **Siletz Tribal Administration and Programs Building**
  (210 SE Swan)
  Headquarters for the Confederated Tribes of the Siletz..

- **Paul Washington Tribal Cemetery** *(Cemetery Road)*
  On the same grounds where Tribal administrative offices are located.

Siletz Grange

Siletz to Kernville

Distance:
 22.9 miles

Directions:
 From the Siletz Grange, proceed west on Highway 229 (Gaither).

Points En Route

(mileage from the Siletz Grange)

2.9 miles:
 Ojalla Bridge. Named for Finnish immigrants who purchased the property in 1907, this is the third bridge spanning the river at this site.

3.9 miles:
 Kosydar Farms, since 1906.

5.9 miles:
 A.W. "Jack" Morgan Park.

9.6 miles:
 Strome Park. Boat launch.

10.9 miles:
 Roots Creek. Named after Thomas A. Roots, the 1897 postmaster of the small, former community that once existed here.

17.1 miles:
 Itchwit Park. Boat launch, restrooms.

17.6 miles:
 Skunk Creek. Named for an episode in which a local settler came out second best following a brief encounter with the cute black and white animal.

20.0 miles:
 Chinook Bend. Named for the great fish once caught in abundance at this point, which is still popular with salmon anglers.

20.9 miles:
 Coyote Rock. Note houses on stilts and the historical marker at this point.

21.6 miles:
 The house across the river was built as a set for the 1971 movie version of Ken Keesey's novel, *Sometimes a Great Notion*. It is now a private residence.

22.1 miles:
 Site of the Kern brothers' cannery. Pilings in the river are remnants of the dock, cannery and warehouse.

22.9 miles:
 Siletz Moorage.

22.9 miles:
 Kernville

Siletz River

Kernville

Elevation: 32 feet

Location:
44.88.602 N • 124.01.033 W

Services:
food

Kernville was named after the Kern brothers, Daniel and John, who came from Portland to operate a salmon cannery near the mouth of the Siletz River. The business opened in 1896 as Kern Brothers Packing Company, the same year the post office opened. Kernville was the first white settlement in North Lincoln County. An early story tells of the Siletz Indians receiving twenty-five cents for each Chinook salmon and ten cents for each Silver salmon they sold to the cannery. The original town of Kernville, complete with a sawmill, post office, and general store, was on the southwest bank of the Siletz about one-mile upstream from today's Highway 101.

Points of Interest

- **Kernville Steak and Seafood**
  (186 Kernville Highway)
  Overlooks the Siletz River.

- **Kernville Bridge** *(Highway 101)*
  This new bridge replaced the one built in 1926. Until the bridge was completed, all supplies were boated upriver.

Kernville Steak and Seafood

Kernville Bridge

Pilings in the Siletz River

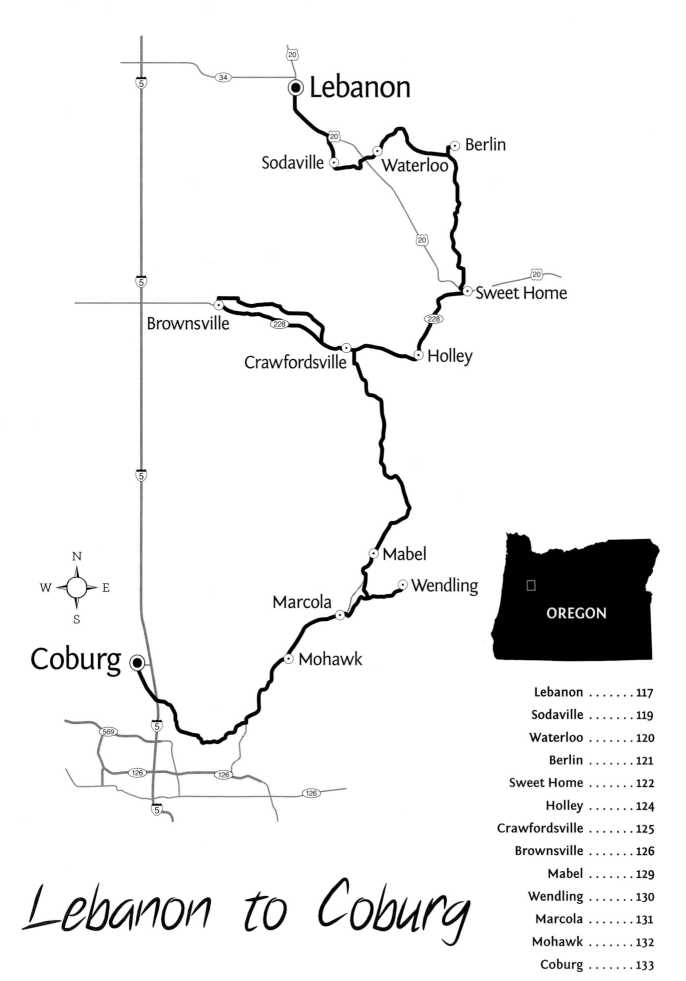

Lebanon

Berlin

Sodaville · Waterloo

Sweet Home

Brownsville

Crawfordsville · Holley

Mabel

Wendling

Marcola

Coburg · Mohawk

OREGON

Lebanon 117

Sodaville 119

Waterloo 120

Berlin 121

Sweet Home 122

Holley 124

Crawfordsville 125

Brownsville 126

Mabel 129

Wendling 130

Marcola 131

Mohawk 132

Coburg 133

Lebanon to Coburg

Meet Your Waterloo near Berlin

Lebanon to Coburg (74 miles)

This route affords a scenic drive through some of Oregon's oldest communities, skirting the foothills of the Cascades where the counties of Linn and Lane greet each other. Five covered bridges are on this tour, two decked with wooden planks. The road wanders through miles of fertile farmland through the communities of Sodaville, once famous for its mineral springs; to Berlin, site of a horse race track; and on to historic Brownsville before ending in Springfield. Farms, mills, streams, forests, and century-old homesteads are the rule rather than the exception along these roads less traveled.

Crawfordsville Covered Bridge

Lebanon

Elevation: 351 feet

Location:
44.32.259 N • 122.54.258 W

Services:
gas, food, lodging

Lebanon was originally known as Peterson's Gap, named after Asa Peterson who settled here in the 1840s. It was also called Kees Station and Kees Precinct, named after 1848 settlers Jacob and Morgan Kees. Jeremiah Ralston surveyed the community in 1851, renaming the community Lebanon after his home in Tennessee. The Lebanon post office opened the same year. A different post office opened in 1851 under the name of Santyam. That name

Lebanon Train Depot

was changed to Washington Butte in 1852 and joined with the Lebanon post office in 1855. The town incorporated in 1878. The railroad came to Lebanon in 1880. The newspaper, the Lebanon Express, published its first paper in 1887. Electricity came to town in 1889 and the first telephones were connected in 1890. The Lebanon Canal was hand dug in 1891 and 1892. The first paper mill operated in 1891. The railroad bridge over the Santiam River was constructed in 1910. Lebanon was a territorial stage stop along the Cascade Wagon Road. Lebanon boasts thirty-eight sites on the Linn County Historical Registry and seven listed on the National Historical Registry. Until 2005, Lebanon was home to one of the last drive-in movie theaters in the state. It was demolished to make room for a Super Wal-Mart despite protests by preservationists. Lebanon was once home of the world's largest plywood mill and is known as an important strawberry producer. The annual Strawberry Festival has been held here since 1909 and boasts "The World's Largest Strawberry Shortcake."

Points of Interest

- **Lebanon City Library** *(626 2nd)*
  Opened in 1913 as the Lebanon Hospital.

- **School Park** *(50 3rd)*
  Built on the site of the 1852 school.

- **Lebanon Train Depot** *(735 3rd)*
  Built in 1908, replacing the 1880 depot.

- **Scroggin Feed and Seed** *(280 W Sherman)*
  Originally John Settle's Grain Warehouse, built circa 1870. Ralph Scroggin was a subsequent early owner.

- **Thad Sterling House** *(310 W Grant)*
  Built circa 1896. Sterling was active in the feedstore in the John Settle Grain Warehouse. He sold the house to Ralph Scroggin, around 1910. Ralph, son of J.P. Scroggin, served as Mayor in the late 1930s and owned the Scroggin Feed Mill.

- **Methodist Episcopal Church** *(90 E Vine)*
  Constructed in 1910.

- **Presbyterian Church** *(145 Ash)*
  The church was established 1881 and the building constructed in 1910.

- **J.P. Scroggin House** *(185 W Ash)*
  Circa 1892. Scroggin ran the Seamore and Scroggin Sawmill and, in 1896, opened the bank later known as the Lebanon National Bank.

- **Lebanon Pioneer Cemetery** *(200 Dodge)*
  The cemetery opened in 1850 when a 13-year old girl was buried there.

- **John Baker House** *(515 E Grant)*
  1895. Baker operated a nearby sawmill.

- **Booth House** (*486 Park*)
  The 1906 home of Lebanon's first doctor.

- **Ralston Square Park** (*925 Park*)
  Spans almost 2.5 acres.

- **John Ralston Cottage** (*481 Main*)
  Ralston was the son of town founder Jeremiah, who built this home in 1887. Note the leaded glass windows.

- **Gem Theater** (*644 Main*)
  Opened in the 1940s.

- **Lebanon Hotel** (*651 and 661 Main*)
  The old hotel was open for business in 1913,

- **Kuhn Theater** (*668 Main*)
  Cap Kuhn owned both the Gem Theater and this theater, which opened in 1936.

- **Courtney Block** (*712 Main*)
  1900 construction.

- **The Garland – Bach Meyer Building** (*748 Main*)
  Built in 1910, this building was

the courthouse until 1918 and from 1919 to 1987, the JC Penney Department Store.

- **Andrews and Hackleman Building** (*780 S Main*)
  The two-story structure opened in 1886. The upstairs served as a Masonic Lodge.

- **First National Bank** (*809 S Main*)
  Built in 1910 and now Wells Fargo Bank.

- **Lebanon Creamery Building** (*853 S Main*)
  1928 construction.

- **City Hall** (*925 S Main*)
  The 1928 building once faced Maple Street.

- **Louis Crandall House** (*959 Main*)
  A 1906 Victorian. Louis and his brother Albert operated the Crandall Brothers Planing Mill that produced high quality furniture and building materials.

- **Elkins Flour Mill** (*Olive and Eaton*)
  This large, three-story flourmill was built between 1871 and 1878. It was constructed without any nails and is located behind Linn-Benton Community College offices.

- **Masonic and IOOF Cemeteries** (*off highway 20 near the north entrance to town*)
  Dramatic tombstones of many of Lebanon's early settlers.

- **Booth Park** (*Grant and Hiatt*)
  A large park with restrooms, playground, and picnic area.

- **River Park** (*Grant and Brewster Road*)
  Boat launch, picnic, restrooms, and fishing.

J.P. Scroggin House

Thad Sterling / Ralph Scroggin House

Lebanon to Sodaville

Distance:
4.1 miles

Directions:
From downtown Lebanon at Oak and Main (Highway 20), drive south on Main.

Points En Route

(mileage from Oak and Main)

1.5 miles:
Weldwood Mill Water Tower.

2.9 miles:
Turn right on Sodaville Road.

4.1 miles:
Sodaville

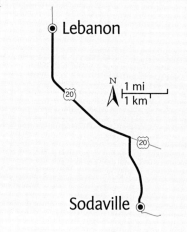

Sodaville

Elevation: 503 feet

Location:
44.48.381 N • 122.52.701 W

Services:
food

Sodaville received its name from the mineral springs found in what is now Sodaville Park. Rueben Coyle discovered the springs in 1848, and the water was eventually bottled and sold, becoming one of the community's major economic endeavors. The post office opened in the 1860s and the city incorporated in 1880. At one time, Sodaville had two colleges — Mineral Springs Seminary in 1892, and Mineral Springs College in 1895. In addition to the colleges, Sodaville had three churches, two hotels, and a meat market, telegraph office, doctor, barber, gunsmith, blacksmith, and livery stable. Many oak trees dot the landscape, and several of the city's streets remain unpaved.

Old Store and Gas Station

Points of Interest

- **Mineral Springs Park**
  (Sodaville Road and Main)
  The park is about one-acre, and the covered mineral spring is its focus. The nearby city hall building was once part of the soda springs bottling works. In the center of the park is a monument to the 1871 parkland donor. An early advertisement for the soda water company read, "These waters have a pungent but not unpleasant taste resembling seltzer." The waters were said to be an aide to diseases of the liver, dyspepsia, and some skin diseases. Bottling water ended in 1953 when tests revealed the water supply to be contaminated.

- **Sodaville City Hall** *(next to the park at Sodaville and Main)*
  Formerly the bottling works.

- **Old Store and Gas Station**
  (*30745 Sodaville Road-across from the Sodaville Store*)
  This building, with its curious construction, has served many purposes over the past ninety years.

- **Old Church** (*30699 Spring*)
  This hundred-year-old structure sits on the side of the hill near the center of the small community.

- **Old House** (*38120 Maple*)
  Turn of the century construction.

- **Old House** (*Maple and Park*)
  The manager of the bottling company once owned this home, built in the early 1900s.

- **Old House** (*Washington and Elm*)
  Another home owned by a bottling works executive.

- **Old Barn** (*Spring and Vine*)
  Unique construction.

- **Sand Ridge Elementary School** (*Sodaville-Mountain Home Road, near Charles Street*)
  This former public school, built in the 1920s, is now a charter school.

Old Barn

Sodaville to Waterloo

Distance:
2.6 miles

Directions:
From the intersection of Main and Sodaville Road, drive up the hill on Main, heading south past city hall.

Points En Route

(mileage from the park at Main and Sodaville)

0.1 miles:
Main becomes Maple.

1.1 miles:
Maple becomes Sodaville-Waterloo Road.

1.9 miles:
Intersection with Highway 20. Cross the highway and stay on Sodaville-Waterloo Drive.

2.0 miles:
Crossing railroad tracks.

2.6 miles:
Waterloo

Waterloo

Elevation: 404 feet

Location:
44.29.401 N • 122.49.333 W

Services:
food, camping, RV

Waterloo gets its name from a tongue-in-cheek dig at a lawsuit brought about after the Kees family, originally from Lebanon and early settlers in the area, leased out their original land claim. The name stuck when one party in the litigation "met their Waterloo" in court, losing a major decision. The post office opened in 1875 and the town was incorporated in 1893.

Points of Interest

- **Waterloo Store** (*7th and Gross*)
  This building once housed the town's mercantile store, feed store, and hardware store.

- **Waterloo County Park**
  (*39510 Gross*)
  Large pieces of basalt form the riverbed here. Waterloo Road divides the park in half with picnic area, restrooms, and fishing access in both sections. The park has year around camping.

Waterloo Store

Waterloo to Berlin

Distance:
4.7 miles

Directions:
From Waterloo Park, at the intersection of 1st and Waterloo Road, cross the bridge and proceed north on Waterloo Road.

Points En Route

(mileage from the bridge)

1.2 miles:
Intersection with Berlin Road; turn right.

1.5 miles:
Mallard Creek Golf Course.

4.0 miles:
Old house.

4.1 miles:
Berlin Church.

4.3 miles:
Intersection with Upper Berlin Ridge Road; turn left.

4.7 miles:
Berlin

Berlin

Elevation: 501 feet

Location:
44.29.881 N • 122.44.806 W

Services:
none

Located on Hamilton Creek, this community was established around a horse racetrack. T. Burrell, a Linn County pioneer, horse breeder, and local racetrack owner, was known for his hospitality during horse races. Attendance at the track was often quite large, so he began charging for meals and lodging. The locale became known as Burrell's Inn, which was shortened to Berlin. The racetrack stood in the field to the left of the farmhouse, which has since been converted from an inn to a private residence. The church on the hill and a few homes along Hamilton Creek are all that remain of this small community. The post office operated from 1899 to 1935. In 1944, during WW II, anti-German forces worked to change the name from Berlin to Distomo, a Greek name. Local citizens rallied and the name remained.

Points of Interest

- **Burrell's Inn** *(41275 Upper Berlin Road - bottom of hill)*
  This was the original farm home of the Burrell family and site of their inn.

- **Gilbert Century Farm** *(41374 Upper Berlin Road)*
  Dates to 1893.

- **Hamilton Creek School** *(3.5 miles west on Berlin Road)*
  The 1894 schoolhouse sits empty in front of the new, modern building. The schools were built near the old dam that used to harness waterpower for a flourmill that stood on the river side of the highway.

Gilbert Century Farm

Berlin to Sweet Home

Distance:
7.4 miles

Directions:
From Burrell's Inn, backtrack to Berlin Road.

Points En Route

(mileage from the original Burrell House)

0.4 miles:
Intersection with Berlin Road. Turn left.

1.1 miles:
Berlin Cemetery. The cemetery dates to the late 1880s.

2.3 miles:
Intersection of Berlin Road and McDowell Creek Road. Stay on Berlin Road.

3.8 miles:
Marksridge Winery.

6.4 miles:
Old school. Turn right onto Pleasant Valley Road.

7.3 miles:
Crossing the Santiam River.

7.4 miles:
Sweet Home

Berlin

Sweet Home

Sweet Home

Elevation: 561 feet

Location:
44.23.732 N • 122.43.192 W

Services:
gas, food, lodging, B&B

The Santiam bands of the Kalapuya Indian Tribe were the area's first residents. The camas plant and antlered game were plentiful and lived peacefully alongside the settlers. The last member of the tribe, Indian Lize, died in 1921. The community of Sweet Home gets its name either from 1850s settlers William Clark and Samuel Powell, who thought it a sweet place to live, or from Lowell Ames, who named it after his favorite song, *Home Sweet Home*. It has been referred to as Mossville, for general store owner Z.B. Moss, and Buck Head, for the elk antlers that adorned Moss's general store. The small post office opened in 1874 and the town incorporated in 1893. A tollbooth once stood a few miles east of town, charging travelers a fee to cross the Cascades. The town slowly grew until the railroad arrived in 1932. Then, with the abundance of timber from local forests, mills sprouted, and freight trains carried millions of board feet of lumber away from the area. As timber played out, the construction of Green Peter Dam and Foster Dam offered new life to the town, providing not only hydroelectric power, but also recreation in the forms of swimming, fishing and boating. Ancient Sweet Home was the site of a huge prehistoric forest, which makes it a great place for rock hounds seeking jasper, agates, fossils, petrified wood, and crystal geodes. Today, farming, lumbering, and tourism turn the wheels of Sweet Home's economy.

East Linn County Museum

Points of Interest

- **Ames Creek**
  (runs through Sweet Home)
  This creek served as the early water source for the community and was named after early settler Lowell Ames.

- **East Linn County Museum**
  (746 Long)
  This 1905 building was first a schoolhouse, then used as a church in the 1940s and converted to a museum in 1970.

Sweet Home

Points of Interest (continued)

- **Sweet Home City Hall** (*1140 12th Avenue*) The old building dates to 1954.

- **Old Church** (*12th and Kalmia*) Now the Hope Center. Unique curved entrance.

- **Sweet Home Library** (*1223 Kalmia*) Built in the 1950s.

- **Rio Theater** (*1439 Main*) Opened in the 1930s.

- **Sweet Home Chamber of Commerce** (*1575 Main*) Information and visitors center.

- **Sankey Park** (*14th and Hawthorne*) The land for the park was donated to the city in 1935, and the structures were built in 1938-39 through WPA funding. Picnic, restrooms, play equipment.

- **Weddle Covered Bridge** (*14th and Kalmia – in Sankey Park*) Named for an early pioneer family, this 1937 bridge was reconstructed on this site after being moved from its original location on Thomas Creek near Gilkey.

- **Dahlenburg Covered Bridge** (*next to the Weddle Covered Bridge*) Used by pedestrians to cross Thomas Creek, this bridge was also moved from its original site.

- **Church of Christ** (*18th and Long*) An impressive structure built in 1906 as an Evangelical Church. The Church of Christ purchased it in 1918 and remodeled it in 1948. Today, it is the Sweet Home Christian Church.

- **Whites Electronics** (*1011 Pleasant Valley Road*) Metal detectors and electronic gadgets. A small museum displays early devices.

- **Short Covered Bridge** (*12.3 miles. Proceed on Highway 20 and turn left onto High Deck Road and continue to milepost 39*) Built in 1945, this is one of the youngest covered bridges in the state.

Weddle Covered Bridge

Dahlenburg Covered Bridge

Sweet Home to Holley

Distance:
4.1 miles

Directions:
At the intersection of Main and Holley (Highway 20 and Highway 228), proceed southwest on Holley.

Points En Route

(mileage from the intersection of Main and Holley)

0.5 miles:
Sweet Home Cemetery. 1863.

2.5 miles:
Greenville Road and site of Greenville. A few homes and barns remain.

3.8 miles:
1929 Holley School.

4.1 miles:
Holley

Holley

Elevation: 534 feet

Location:
44.35.430 N • 122.78.311 W

Services:
gas, food

A settler in 1890 named Holley after his native home in Wisconsin, though some say the name comes from the Oregon grape that grows abundantly in the area and that the early settler mistook for holly. The community today consists of a school, store, church, grange, and a few houses.

Points of Interest

- **Holley Grange #325**
  (Holley Heights Loop)
  The grange was built in the 1920s and held many dances and pie socials through the years.

- **Holley Christian Church**
  (40346 Highway 228)
  Founded in 1871, this church was built in 1897.

- **Calapooia** *(2.8 miles south and east on Upper Calapooia River Road)*
  Named for the Native Americans that lived in the area. En route, look for the 1853 Rice Century Farm, the 1868 home, and the 1920s Calapooia School, now a private residence.

Holley Grange

Rice Century Farm

Holley to Crawfordsville

Distance:
3.1 miles

Directions:
From the Holley Store, proceed west on Highway 228 towards Crawfordsville.

Points En Route

(mileage from the Holley Store)

2.8 miles:
Crawfordsville Cemetery, dating to 1852.

3.1 miles:
Crawfordsville

Crawfordsville

228

Holley

N 2000 ft 500 m

Crawfordsville

Elevation: 461 feet

Location:
44.21.252 N • 122.51.281 W

Services:
gas, food

Crawfordsville was named in honor of Philemon Crawford, a pioneer from Indiana who, in 1851, donated the land for the town. The post office opened in 1870 and Jasper Crawford, Philemon's son, served as the community's first postmaster. Although Crawfordsville was officially platted in 1870, it never incorporated.

Crawfordsville Market

Points of Interest

- **Crawfordsville Market**
  (38396 Highway 228)
  An old convenience store.

- **Crawfordsville Café**
  (38380 Highway 228)
  Constructed in 1890, this building was once a two-story general store. Closed.

- **Crawfordsville School**
  (on Glass between 1st and 2nd)
  Opened in the 1910s.

- **Crawfordsville Covered Bridge** *(off of Highway 228)*
  This 1936 bridge, now closed to car traffic, spans the Calapooia River.

- **Old House** *(next to the bridge at 38289 Courtney Road)*
  More than 100-years old, a newer addition doubled its size.

Crawfordsville to Brownsville

Distance:
6.0 miles

Directions:
From the bridge, proceed west on Highway 228 towards Brownville.

Points En Route

(mileage from the covered bridge)

0.4 miles:
Finley Pioneer Cemetery.

0.7 miles:
McKercher County Park.

4.4 miles:
Wheeler Farm.

5.6 miles:
Altavista B&B and Century Farm (35580 Highway 228).

The home was built in 1876 by Hugh Brown, founder of Brownsville.

6.0. miles:
Brownsville

Brownsville

228

N
1 mi
1 km

Crawfordsville

Brownsville

Elevation: 535 feet

Location:
44.23.367 N • 122.59.111 W

Services:
gas, food, lodging, B&B, camping

Brownsville was settled in 1846 when several families (Browns, Kirks and Blakelys) joined to form this community on the Calapooia River, which split into the two separate towns of North Brownsville and Amelia. Alexander Kirk built a hand hauled ferry that connected the two communities in 1847, until a covered bridge was constructed in 1853. A dam was built three miles upriver, and a ditch (millrace) was hand dug to supply reliable waterpower for industry in the new town. The first business on the millrace was a gristmill, followed by a woolen mill and then a sawmill, furniture factory, and tannery. The railroad came to the area in 1880, which formed a bustling manufacturing and trade center, and the two communities consolidated in 1895 under the name Brownsville. In 1919, a fire destroyed many downtown businesses. The town quickly rebuilt, using brick as the main material for construction. This picturesque settlement, nestled into the foothills of the Cascades, continues to be home to people who take pride in their historic town and who value its past and peaceful, small town atmosphere. Brownsville hosts the Linn County Pioneer Picnic, Oregon's oldest continuing celebration since the first reunion of Oregon Trail pioneers in 1887. An annual Antique Faire draws dealers and collectors from the entire Willamette Valley. The Willamette Country Music Festival is Oregon's fastest growing outdoor music and camping event. Brownsville was the site of the 1985 movie, *Stand By Me*.

Moyer House

Points of Interest

- **Brownsville Christian Church** (*117 N Main*)
  Founded in 1868, this building was constructed in 1895.

- **Moyer House** (*204 N Main*)
  Built in 1881 and open for visitors.

- **Brownsville City Hall** (*255 N Main*)
  Constructed in the 1940s.

- **Pioneer Picture Gallery** (*258 N Main*)
  Originally a mortuary.

- **Bank of Brownsville** (*333 N Main*)
  The former bank opened in 1903.

- **Corner Café** (*421 N Main*)
  Originally the 1874 Starr and Blakely Drugstore. It is the oldest wooden commercial building in town.

- **IOOF Lodge #43 Building** (*Main*)
  Built of brick in 1908.

- **L.C. Rice House** (*730 N Main*)
  Constructed in 1875.

- **Cavendar-Goshow House** (*804 N Main*)
  Built in 1893.

- **Brownsville City Park** (*Park Avenue*)
  The site of the annual Linn County Pioneer Picnic. A monument to the pioneers, placed by the Linn County Pioneer Association, is at the corner of Fisher and Park. Picnic, camping, restrooms, playground.

Brownsville

Points of Interest (continued)

- **Five Houses** (*Walnut*)
  Each home is similarly designed and built between 1908 and 1910.

- **Train Depot** (*Depot Avenue*)
  Site of the old train depot, which was moved to 101 Park.

- **Old House** (*608 Oak*)
  An 1850's home built in the Greek Revival style and moved to this location.

- **William Beyer House** (*619 Oak*)
  Built in 1889.

- **Martha Beyer House** (*627 Oak*)
  1870s.

- **Cox-Stanard House** (*704 Oak*)
  Circa 1882.

- **Pillsbury-Brown House** (*721 Oak*)
  Constructed in 1887 and purchased by F.F. Brown in 1903. His name is etched into the picture window.

- **Brownsville Baptist Church** (*515 N Main*)
  Built in 1906 on the site of the 1865 church.

- **R.H. and Emma Carl House** (*711 Main*)
  1890 Italianate construction.

- **Ross/H.J.C. Averill House** (*420 Averill*)
  This large home was built in 1867.

- **A. Marster House** (*504 Averill*)
  Constructed in 1876.

- **Masonic Lodge #36** (*113-114 Stanard*)
  Founded in 1865. The Pearly-Webber building was constructed in 1903 and was Brownsville's first brick building. The building was occupied by the Woodsmen of the World (#214) from 1903 to 1937, and by the Masons from 1937 until 2003.

- **C.J. Howe Building** (*104 Spaulding*)
  1908.

- **Blakely-Simmons House** (*229 Spalding*)
  1865 construction.

- **J.F. Venner House** (*232 Spaulding*)
  Built in 1898.

Brownsville Christian Church

Masonic Lodge

- **W.J. Moore House** (*305 Kirk*)
  1893.

- **J.B. Moore House** (*320 Kirk*)
  1893.

- **C.J. Howe House** (*331 Kirk*)
  Constructed in 1911.

- **S.A. Kirk House** (*352 Kirk*)
  1895.

- **A.L. Kirk House** (*355 Kirk*)
  Built in 1892.

- **Presbyterian Church**
  (*Washburn and Vroman*)
  The church was established in 1857 and this building constructed in 1896.

- **Union Point**
  (*2.9 miles on Gap Road*)
  Site of the 1854 Union Point post office. A historical marker tells the early history of Union Point. The old Union Point School, now a private residence, stands nearby.

Brownsville to Mabel

Distance:
19.6 miles

Directions:
From the intersection of Kirk and Main, drive east on Kirk.

Points En Route

(mileage from the intersection of Kirk and Main)

0.7 miles:
1895 Jacob Wigle Farmstead and Hop Barn with cupola.

0.9 miles:
Intersection of Kirk and Northern Drive. Turn right on Northern.

1.8 miles:
Old farm with weathervane.

6.4 miles:
Northern Drive intersects with Highway 228. Turn left on Highway 228.

7.0 miles:
Finley Pioneer Cemetery.

7.4 miles:
Entering Crawfordsville. Continue through town.

8.0 miles:
Turn right on Brush Creek Road, also known as the Marcola Highway.

14.2 miles:
Entering Lane County.

19.6 miles:
Mabel

Brownsville Train Depot

Jacob Wigle Hop Barn

Mabel

Elevation: 614 feet

Location:
44.21.519 N • 122.82.693 W

Services:
none

Mabel had its beginning in 1870, when a small group of settlers cleared the virgin Douglas Fir forest to build a sawmill above the entrance of Shotgun Creek where it empties into the Mohawk River. By 1878, a community had developed around the mill. Alfred Drury established a post office in 1878, served as the first postmaster and named the little town after his daughter. The post office closed in 1957. A large population of Japanese Americans lived here in the 1920s. Many mill sites can be seen in the area. A few homes and barns make up this small settlement today, a skeleton of what it was in its heyday.

Points of Interest

- **Mohawk Grange** (*near the Mabel community marker; follow the local road a hundred yards to the grange*) Situated on the Mohawk River, this grange was the former 1890 Mohawk Valley School.

- **Gus and Mabel Alexander House** (*across from the entrance to the street that leads to the grange*) Mabel, for whom the community was named, and her husband built this home in 1913. Shortly thereafter, they moved to Beaverton where Gus was elected city recorder in 1918 and again from 1921-1929. Mabel was appointed elections clerk in 1916 and served in that capacity from 1921-1926 and 1929-1930.

Gus and Mabel Alexander House

Mabel to Wendling

Distance:
4.1 miles

Directions:
From the Gus Alexander House, continue west on Marcola Road.

Points En Route

(*mileage from the Alexander House*)

1.0 miles:
Turn left on Paschelke Road.

1.1 miles:
Earnest Covered Bridge. This 1938 bridge spans the Mohawk River. Continue on Paschelke Road. The 1965 movie *Shenandoah*, starring Jimmy Stewart, was filmed here in 1965.

1.3 miles:
J Bar C Ranch.

2.3 miles:
92639 Paschelke Road. A barn converted into a house.

2.4 miles:
Turn left on Wendling Road.

3.9 miles:
Tipi Village Retreat Center.

4.1 miles:
Wendling

Wendling

Elevation: 631 feet

Location:
44.11.438 N • 122.47.816 W

Services:
none

In 1899, the post office opened in this mill town named for George Wendling, director of the Booth-Kelley Lumber Company. By 1903, Wendling had a school, church, and a resident doctor. A stagecoach connected Springfield and Wendling with three-trips a day service. By 1908, Wendling had prospered and grown large enough to have a train depot, locomotive barn, bakery, machine shop, billiard and card room, confectionary, barber shop, skating rink, two churches and three bowling alleys. A fire in 1910 did considerable damage to the community, burning most of the businesses and homes, but sparing the mill. The community was rebuilt, only to have a second fire destroy the mill in 1924. Even though rebuilt, the Great Depression and over-cutting of timber brought the community to it knees. As lumber production slowed, the small community began to die. By 1952 the post office closed, timber was depleted, and the land sold. Pieces of the wooden log flume and a child's cemetery, miles above the former community, are said to exist today.

Points of Interest

- **Wendling Covered Bridge**
  (spans Mill Creek)
  This 1938 bridge once carried numerous log trucks and workers to the expansive mill.

- **Wendling Homestead**
  (39837 Wendling Road)
  One of the few homes remaining in this former mill town.

Wendling Covered Bridge

Wendling to Marcola

Distance:
3.4 miles

Directions:
From the covered bridge, travel south and return to the intersection of Wendling and Paschelke.

Points En Route

(mileage from the covered bridge)

1.8 miles:
Intersection with Wendling and Paschelke. Stay on Wendling.

2.1 miles:
An old barn that has been converted to a residence.

3.2 miles:
The remodeled Mohawk High School and a century-old farmhouse.

3.4 miles:
Marcola

Marcola

Elevation: 531 feet

Location:
44.10.342 N • 122.51.473 W

Services:
gas, food

First known as Isabel, the post office opened in 1876, named for the wife of an early settler. In 1900, when the railroad came through the Mohawk Valley, the name was changed. The name Marcola comes from combining the first and last names of Mary Cole, the wife of the town's founder. The Marcola post office opened in 1901. To the west lie the Coburg Hills, with Camp Creek Ridge forming the eastern valley wall. The minor streams of McGowan Creek, Parson Creek, Mill Creek, Cartwright Creek, and Cash Creek all drain into the Mohawk River and have helped form this river valley. Marcola celebrates Mary Cole Days the last week of July every year.

Cole House

Points of Interest

• **Cole House**
  (corner of Whitmore and Marcola Road)
  This was the 1889 home of the town founder.

• **Dewilt Home**
  (92175 Marcola Highway)
  Across the street from the Cole House, this old home has an unusual arbor entrance.

Marcola to Mohawk

Distance:
3.6 miles

Directions:
From the intersection of Whitmore and Marcola Road (the Cole House), go west on Marcola Road toward Springfield.

Points En Route

(mileage from the Cole House)

0.5 miles:
1880s Marcola Cemetery.

2.1 miles:
Turn right on Donna Road and drive west.

3.4 miles:
The 1917 Donna School, now a private residence.

3.6 miles:
Mohawk

Mohawk

Elevation: 505 feet

Location:
44.08.508 N • 122.54.590 W

Services:
gas, food

Jacob C. Spores, an early settler who operated a ferry on the McKenzie River, named the area in honor of the New York river he fondly remembered (*Mohawk* translates into 'eaters of live meat'). The Mohawk post office opened in 1862 and closed in 1961. The 1914 store and the 1917 Donna School are the key holdovers from the early settlement. A few scattered homes from the original community still stand in the area.

Mohawk Trading Post and Store

Points of Interest

- **Mohawk Trading Post and Store** (*Hill and Donna*)
  Open since 1914.

- **Mohawk (Donna) School** (*91217 Donna*)
  The 1917 school is now a private residence.

- **Mohawk Cemetery** (*90702 Hill Road*)
  Dates to the 1870s.

Mohawk to Coburg

Distance:
11.5 miles

Directions:
From the intersection of Hill and Donna, drive southwest on Hill Road.

Points En Route

(mileage from the Mohawk Store)

1.2 miles:
Valley View Cemetery, 1870s.

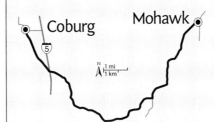

3.9 miles:
Turn right on McKenzie View Road, traveling toward Coburg. The road will parallel the McKenzie River.

7.9 miles:
Old farmstead with unique water tower.

9.9 miles:
Intersection of McKenzie View Road and Coburg Road. Turn right on Coburg Road.

10.7 miles:
The 1882 IOOF Cemetery.

11.5 miles:
Coburg

Coburg

Elevation: 400 feet

Location:
44.08.141 N • 122.03.492 W

Services:
gas, food, lodging. B&B

Coburg was first settled in 1847 by John Diamond and Jacob Spores and was originally called Diamond. The name was changed to Coburg in 1865 for a stallion imported from Coburg, Germany. John Diamond, an early Oregon Explorer, is credited with climbing and naming Diamond Peak and Diamond Lake. The first school in Coburg opened in 1865, the narrow gauge railroad came to town in 1878, and the town incorporated in 1893. In 1900, the Booth-Kelley Mill opened operations, then closed in 1912 when fire destroyed the plant. Another fire, in 1915, burned four blocks of homes and businesses in the city center. Coburg is recognized as a National Historic District, encompassing more than 187 structures and sites with twenty historic homes exhibiting a variety of architectural styles common to the late 1800's. Charming Coburg hosts an annual Antique Faire on the first Sunday after Labor Day that draws over 350 antique dealers from over six states to the streets of the downtown area. In addition to its many antique shops, Coburg is home to Monaco Motor Coaches, a manufacturer of upscale motor homes.

Depot House

Points of Interest

- **Goodman House**
  (91131 N Diamond)
  1900 construction.

- **Diamond House**
  (91143 N Diamond)
  The town founder's home, built in 1889.

- **William Van Duyn House**
  (91108 N Willamette)
  This 1877 home has also been an Inn and Restaurant.

- **IOOF Hall** *(91119 N Willamette)*
  Burned in 1938, rebuilt in 1941.

- **Drury House** *(91157 N Diamond)*
  More than a century old.

- **Allingham House**
  (91163 N Willamette)
  Built about 1897.

- **J.C. Goodale House**
  (91177 N Willamette)
  Circa 1890.

- **Brockway House**
  (91129 N Miller)
  Constructed in 1909.

- **Wilkins-Seary House**
  (91212 N Miller)
  A farm in 1902.

- **Bartholomew House**
  (32666 Locust)
  This home was built about 1900.

- **Coburg Grange Hall**
  (32663 E Mill)
  1920s.

- **Clark-Moser House**
  (32756 E Mill)
  The Clark home was built about 1895.

- **Smith House** *(32677 E McKenzie)*
  Known as the Depot House, circa 1870.

- **Coburg Christian Church**
  (32694 Pearl)
  Constructed in 1904, the large church sits vacant.

- **Coburg Bed and Breakfast** (*32712 E McKenzie*)
  A restored 1880s farmhouse.

- **Samuel Matthews House** (*32702 E Pearl*)
  Built in 1905, it is now an antique store.

- **Hullin House** (*32713 E Dixon*)
  Circa 1901.

- **Chandler House** (*32752 Dixon*)
  1902 construction.

- **Anderson House** (*32801 E Maple*)
  Circa 1899.

- **Green House** (*90972 S Coleman*)
  Circa 1901.

- **Healy House** (*91020 S Willamette*)
  1898.

- **Pollard House** (*91032 S Willamette*)
  The oldest home in Coburg, built in 1854.

- **Payne House** (*91035 S Willamette*)
  Built in 1905.

- **Coburg City Park** (*Willamette and Harrison*)
  Covers several blocks.

- **Purkerson House** (*91045 S Willamette*)
  Constructed in 1890.

- **Mendanhall House** (*91049 S Willamette*)
  Built in 1905, it is now a beauty shop.

Diamond House

Coburg Bed and Breakfast

Samuel Matthews House

134

About the Author

Author Steve Arndt grew up in rural Independence, Oregon during the state's centennial, a setting that kindled his curiosity about the region's history.

His uncle, William Gilbaugh, now a retired Washington State park ranger and noted northwest photographer, further ignited his passion by occasionally taking Steve on tours of Oregon and Washington back roads and byways.

After earning a degree in elementary education from Oregon College of Education (now Western Oregon University), Steve completed advanced degree coursework in special education at OCE, school administration at Portland State University, and his school superintendent credentials at the University of Oregon. In his 40-year career in education, Steve served various Oregon public schools as teacher and administrator, and completed his last nineteen years in higher education as senior associate professor of teacher education, including ten years as a department chair.

Steve, his wife Diane, and their now-grown children have spent many weekends and school vacations exploring Oregon back roads and off-the-beaten places. Today, their car is filled with child safety seats for young granddaughters that have begun road-trips with grandma and grandpa.

Both Steve and Diane continue to fill important roles at the Woodburn United Methodist Church and enjoy volunteering in the Woodburn community and participating in various philanthropic groups and endeavors.

Although Diane, a retired music educator and professional singer, has no formal training in photography, she enjoys her role as photographer, organizer, and proofreader of Steve's book series.